W9-DBM-024

Intermittent Fasting for Women

Lose Weight, Balance Your Hormones, and Boost Anti-Aging with the Power of Autophagy – 16/8, One Meal a Day, 5:2 Diet, and More!

Table of Contents

Introduction

Intermittent fasting has gained popularity in recent years. Hundreds of books and articles have already been written about it. No one can blame these authors since it is a revolutionary way of achieving weight loss. There is no diet. All you have to do is time when you eat and do not eat. Unfortunately, a lot of the information written were created with a male audience or men and women, in general, in mind.

This is where the problem becomes evident. What is written for men rarely applies to women. The body of a man works different to that of a woman and vice versa. Therefore, it is only natural for women to react differently to intermittent fasting. And, as you would find out, this is actually the case.

Moreover, given that there's a difference with how it affects men and women, the methods, tips, and solutions written for men might not actually be effective for women. Women might actually be placing their health at risk by following advice meant for the opposite sex.

It is for this reason that this book was written. This book aims to look at intermittent fasting and see how it can specifically affect women. It looks into the effects and benefits for their health. It would also look into how women can do intermittent fasting in a way that suits them best.

Aside from this, this book would delve deeper into the aspects of intermittent fasting. There a lot of talk about its effects on weight and fat loss. But, it is rarely discussed that intermittent fasting can do so much more than just helping people lose weight. In fact, with its potential benefits for your health, it can be said that everyone should actually do intermittent fasting using one of the methods available.

Why?

Intermittent fasting triggers a reaction in your body that is essential to its survival, longevity, and overall health. From a book wherein its audience would probably expect to talk only about fat loss, this book goes so much deeper that it delves into disease prevention, mental enhancement, and potential degenerative disease treatment. Of course, proper research was done to ensure that what is provided in this book can be applied to your life.

Furthermore, this book will provide you with the tools to implement the strategy that will help you have an easier time achieving your goal. It will also clarify some misunderstandings about it and fix some misconceptions about intermittent fasting, weight loss, and diet. It will also provide information on what you need to get started and why you need them.

After reading this book, you will have a better understanding of intermittent fasting, its mechanics, and its actual method. You will also have an idea on how you can do intermittent fasting in a way that works best for your physiology, health condition, preferences, and lifestyle. You will even be given a guide on how to make intermittent fasting easier or, at the very least, more manageable for you. You will also be equipped on how to go about when changing your goals.

From all of these, you will know everything you need to know to get started with intermittent fasting immediately. The only thing missing is for you to start and take action.

The Basics About Intermittent Fasting

Fasting is nothing new. You probably have heard of various cultures and religions with practices that willingly restrain or reduce their consumption of all or certain types of drink, food, or both, for a given amount of time. You might have also experienced, or know someone who has, fasting as a way to prepare for a surgery or a medical test.

What is not common is willingly fasting on a regular basis for weight loss. Such practices are often compared to alternative medicine practices that have a reputation for having no scientific basis. In some cases, it is even viewed as unhealthy.

However, this is not the case for intermittent fasting. Although it would trigger a fasted state, your body would still get the macro and micronutrients it needs to maintain its health and functions. This results in weight loss that does not come with negative health effects for you.

What Is Intermittent Fasting?

Intermittent fasting is different from the usual diet plan that focuses on the caloric content or macronutrient type of your food choices. It focuses more on when you can eat to create the effects that it can cause to your body. Instead, intermittent fasting would have you follow a dieting pattern involving alternating phases of fasting and eating.

During the fasting phase, you are restricted from eating anything that contains calories. It is only during the eating phase that you can consume food or drink containing calories.

Contrary to popular belief, intermittent fasting alone does not directly cause weight loss. It is still caused by the caloric deficit, which is brought about by the fewer meals that arise from the limited time you have for eating. However, unlike diets that solely rely on caloric deficit, it is more sustainable in the long term, more satisfying, and more flexible.

This focus on when you eat your food instead of what you eat gives intermittent fasting its simplicity. You do not have to count calories for every meal. You do not have to restrict your food choices. And, you do not have to follow a meal plan with stringent macronutrient portions.

The Different Ways You Can Do Intermittent Fasting

16/8 method

This is the most popular approach to intermittent fasting. It involves a fasting phase of 16 hours and an eating phase of 8 hours within a single day. This means, if you start your eating phase at 11 in the morning, you will stop eating and start fasting at 7 in the evening. The said fasting phase would then end at 11AM on the next day.

You are free to set the time for your eating and fasting phase. This makes it easy for you to tailor your own intermittent fasting plan to a schedule that would work best for your lifestyle.

The lean gains method falls under this approach. It has the same 16 hours of fasting and 8 hours of eating. However, it was designed for those with a highly active lifestyle such as athletes, weight trainers, and fitness enthusiasts.

The lean gains method places an importance on caloric intake for better fat loss and, at the same time, muscle gain. It also has recommendations on which macronutrient and how much caloric intake work best for the first meal after fasting, pre-workout meals, or rest day meals.

Eat-stop-eat method

The eat-stop-eat method involves a fasting phase that lasts for 24 hours. This 24-hour fasting phase would be done twice per week.

The key to this method is that there should be a meal at least once every day. This means that you should have had eaten a meal before starting a 24-hour fasting phase that starts, for example, at 9 in the morning.

Like the 16/8 method, you can set the start of your fasting phase whenever you want. But, most people following this method choose to set their fasting period from 6PM until 6PM of the next day. This way they do not sleep hungry, which would often be the case for those just starting intermittent fasting.

5:2 method

The 5:2 method derives its name from the five days of normal eating and the two days of fasting involved for a single week. Unlike the other methods, this method does not involve a complete restriction from food during the fasting phases. Instead, the fasting phases come in the form of restricting food intake to 25 percent of a person's daily calorie intake.

These calorie-restricted days can be scheduled whichever day that you want. However, there should always be at least a single day of normal eating between the fasting days.

There is no restriction on one's food choices during the fasting days. There is also no limit on the number of meals in it as long as the total calories does not exceed the limit. Like the modified approach to alternate day fasting, you can spread out the calories for the day to two to three meals.

The common practice for this method is to schedule the fasted days during the weekdays. In this way, they would not be missing out on social events where food is likely involved.

Alternate day fasting (ADF)

The alternate day fasting, or ADF, involves a full day of fasting every other day. This method could be done by a fast that starts the moment you wake up until the time you wake up the next day, or by starting to fast in the evening and ending it after 24 hours. Unlike the eat stop eat method, you will be fasting every other day.

With this method, you are encouraged to drink as much calorie-free beverage that you can. This would include water, and unsweetened tea and coffee. Some would argue that the tea and coffee should have no dairy as well since these contain sugars that your body converts to calories.

You can modify this method so it does not involve a complete restriction from food during the fasting phase. Instead, you can limit your total caloric limit to 25 to 30 percent of your daily calories spread out to two to three meals within the day. In this way, you can stave off the feeling of hunger but still remain on a fasted state. Unlike the two day low calorie fasts of the 5:2 method, you will eat a low amount of calories on alternating days of the week.

The Warrior Diet

The Warrior Diet is called such due to the belief that it was how ancient Paleolithic humans ate at the time. This diet involves a fasting phase of little to no food during the day and an eating phase of consuming as much food as desired.

The fasting phase starts from the moment of waking up during the day. It would last for 20 hours wherein it is encouraged to consume dairy products, raw fruits and vegetables, eggs, and non-caloric beverages in small amounts.

Once the 20-hour fasting phase ends, you are free to "feast" as much as you desire. This eating phase is said to be patterned after how the Spartan and Roman warriors would feast at night after a hard day's work.

As the name implies, the Warrior Diet goes beyond the simple eating and fasting schedule of the other intermittent fasting methods. It involves an actual diet that aims to improve the body's utilization of fat for its metabolism.

Also, it is encouraged for the one following it to take daily multivitamins, probiotics, and amino acids. It is also said to work best while doing a workout plan for increasing strength and speed to lose as much fat as possible during the diet's duration.

One Meal a Day (OMAD)

The One Meal a Day method utilizes a 23-hour fasting phase and a 1-hour eating phase. This would be just enough for you to have a single meal each day. It is a more advanced method compared to the Warrior Diet. You would also be more likely eating less calories in it since you only have an hour to eat.

How Intermittent Fasting Affects Your Body

Intermittent fasting gained its popularity for its simplicity. You just have to follow a schedule on when you can eat and when you cannot. What's great about this simplicity is that it works.

Furthermore, the effects of intermittent fasting goes beyond weight loss. It also has positive effects to the hormones and cells that play a role in your overall and long-term health.

Here are some of the hormones, organs, and cells that intermittent fasting affects that, in turn, contribute to your overall health.

Decreased insulin levels and resistance

Insulin is a hormone produced by the pancreas. It is released when your blood sugar rises. Once released, it triggers the cells to absorb blood sugar. The cells would then use them for energy or, in the case of fat cells, store them for later use.

Insulin is a crucial hormone in the body's moderation of its blood sugar levels. It prompts the liver if there is too much of it to prevent complications arising from hyperglycemia like cardiovascular disease, and damage on the nerves and kidneys.

Unfortunately, we often experience high blood sugar because of the carbohydrate-rich nature of today's diet. This causes frequent spikes in insulin levels that eventually lead to the body developing insulin resistance. This increased resistance results to the body requiring higher levels of insulin to regulate its' blood sugar levels.

This high insulin resistance would eventually manifest in a variety of symptoms such as fatigue, increased belly fat, elevated fasting blood sugar, high blood pressure, and carbohydrate cravings. For women, it could even cause acquired polycystic ovarian syndrome and hair loss.

This body's abnormal resistance to the hormone can be broken through fasting. This is due to the practice of increasing the production of proteins that improve insulin sensitivity.

This was observed from a group of Muslims fasting during the season of Ramadan (1). The good news is that you do not need to follow their practice of fasting from dawn to sunset for 30 days. You can replicate the same results through the easier and shorter fasting regimen that intermittent fasting can provide.

Increased human growth hormone production

Human growth hormone plays a role in inducing growth during childhood, and reaches its peak production during one's teenage years. This slowly declines with age, but it still plays a role in the body's tissue repair, energy, metabolism, brain function and muscle growth. It is produced by your pituitary gland, the pea-sized gland found at the lower part of your brain.

The body increases the production of growth hormone during fasted states while asleep or awake (2, 3, 4). This increase is caused by the decline in the released insulin six hours after eating a meal. Growth hormone levels start to increase after 6 more hours and reach the highest amounts around 18 to 20 hours into the fast. This increase can go up to as much as 2000% as one's average levels and can last for up to 48 hours.

Improved cellular repair

Fasting is among the ways to trigger autophagy in the body. Autophagy is the self-cleaning process done by cells to break down and recycle its damaged organelles and molecules. Although it is a constant process, autophagy increases dramatically when the body's insulin level drops during a fasted state.

The increased cell repair during a fasted state is believed to be the cause of the increased longevity among humans and other organisms that consume a low caloric diet. It arises from how stem cells can regain their regenerative ability through cellular repair. This results to stem cells being able to recover the damage to tissue at a rate that was only possible at a younger age (5).

Improved resistance from oxidative damage

Free radicals occur naturally in the body because of the various metabolic processes in it or the exposure from external sources. The antioxidants produced by your body and obtained from your diet neutralize these to prevent damage to the molecules that make up your cells.

Unfortunately, there will be cases wherein the body has an excess amount of free radicals. This could even be the norm for those who have a poor diet or lifestyle that both contribute to low levels of antioxidants. In such cases, the cells suffer from chronic oxidative stress that leads to damage to their structures. If left unchecked, it could trigger conditions such as heart disease, diabetes, chronic inflammation, neurodegenerative diseases, and cancer.

Fasting can address this and even improve the body's resistance to oxidative damage. This is thanks to the increased production of the gene SIRT3 (6). This gene helps prevent the production of free radicals and improve the processes that reverse the damage done on the cells and its organelles.

Improved heart health

The increased insulin levels brought about by chronically high blood sugar and insulin resistance increases the risk for developing cardiovascular disease. This risk further increases when combined with the complications brought about by the same conditions – obesity and high cholesterol levels.

As previously mentioned, a fasted state will dramatically decrease one's insulin levels. If done consistently through an intermittent fasting schedule, it can eventually bring one's insulin sensitivity back to normal levels. With the improved insulin sensitivity, one can reach a healthier weight, lower their body fat composition, and reduce their blood cholesterol levels. Since these markers have improved, there is a lower chance for heart disease as well.

Better brain function

The improved moderation of blood sugar levels, and reduced oxidative stress and inflammation brought about by intermittent fasting can also improve your brain function. This is due to the neurons switching from cell growth and reproduction to resource conservation and stress resistance. When this happens, the cells remove damaged molecules and dysfunctional organelles. This results to cells with better quality. These neurons would then reproduce when they shift back to growing and reproducing once you eat after fasting.

Also, fasting increases the levels of a hormone known as brain-derived neurotrophic factor (BDNF) (7). This hormone is a critical component in the brain for learning, memory storage and recall, and neuron generation. Also, it helps brain cells to be resistant to stress caused by free radicals, fatigue, and your environment.

Possible prevention of chronic diseases related to cell health

The wastes, damaged molecules, and dysfunctional organelles, especially the mitochondria, increase the risk for diseases such as cancer, Alzheimer's and Parkinson's. With fasting triggering autophagy, these unwanted elements in your cells are flushed out. This could possibly be the reason why fasting has been observed to provide nerves with protection from mechanisms that cause Alzheimer's disease (8). In addition, it has been observed that short-term fasting can improve the effects of cancer treatment while improving the patient's tolerance against chemotherapy (9).

Better gene expression

Gene expression is the process of converting instructions found in our DNA into a useable product. This is what gives our cells the capability to respond to the different changes that happen in our environment. The responses often result in the form of proteins that would then trigger functions within the cell. Examples of these functions include immune response to a bacterial infection, protective response to a detected disease, and hormonal response to changes inside or outside the body.

The numerous gene expressions that happen in our different cells can degrade due to inflammation, oxidative stress, aging, and toxins. This degradation can sometimes lead to the onset of age-related and chronic illnesses and symptoms.

Intermittent fasting has been found to induce changes in the gene expressions. These changes have been noticed to improve the malformed gene expressions that increase the risk for chronic illnesses like heart disease (10), ischemic stroke (11), and metabolic disorders (12).

Less hunger and more satiety for certain individuals

Your body feels hunger and satiety due to the hormones released by your body. The one that makes you feel hungry is known as ghrelin while the hormone that makes you feel full is leptin. These hormones are produced from your stomach and fat cells when certain conditions are met.

Women experience an increase in the production of appetite suppressing hormones while going through a schedule of long-term fasting (13). However, this decrease is not observed among men with healthy body compositions. In fact, leptin decreases after undergoing a schedule of intermittent fasting.

Moreover, women are more likely to maintain their weight after returning to their regular eating schedule. This is attributed to the higher levels of the hormone suppressing the appetite that resulted from intermittent fasting (14).

Before You Get Started

It may seem that you can immediately start to intermittently fast after reading the first chapter of this book. After all, it only involves knowing when to stop and start eating during the day. How hard can it be, right?

This thought is where most people start to do more harm than good to themselves in doing intermittent fasting.

Individuals will have varying experiences while doing an intermittent fast. Because of this, it is easy to miss important information, especially if you are only depending on other people's experiences and advice. Their experiences are dependent on their unique situation and more often, yours are different from theirs.

This is evident with how a woman's reproductive system responds to certain forms of fasting. Women will experience disruptions in their menstrual cycle and a decrease in their fertility with certain types of fasts. According to research, this is due to the increased production of the stress hormone cortisol, and the disruption of sleeping patterns (15).

These effects can be properly addressed with adequate caloric and nutritional intake from meals. But, for those uninformed about this, they could be disheartened by the experience, especially if they are trying to get pregnant while doing this. Furthermore, it could lead to complications if they already have existing health issues.

This is why it is important to get all the facts straight before starting an intermittent fasting schedule. It is also crucial to seek the advice of your doctor before proceeding with any fasting schedule written in this book. A doctor's expert opinion is even more important for those with existing eating disorders, since fasting will cause changes with the hormones related to their appetite.

The Science on Why Intermittent Fasting IS more than just weight loss

The body is in a growth state as long as it is well-fed. Through the action of the hormone insulin and the mTOR (mammalian target of rapamycin) pathways, genes associated with cell survival and reproduction are activated. This results to synthesizing the proteins necessary for your cells to grow and divide themselves. This cellular state of growth and reproduction turns off genes that are contrary to this state. In particular, these genes are the ones responsible for fat metabolism, damage repair, and stress resistance.

When you start a fasting phase, you are setting up the conditions required to deactivate this growth state that your cells are going through. Your blood sugar starts to decrease as your cells continue to use them even without the continuous supply of calories from food. Eventually, your body will run out of glucose. This will start a state wherein the body will start to look for a fuel source other than glucose.

This state is ketosis. While in this state, the body would start metabolizing its fat stores. However, glucose is still an energy requirement for some cells in your body, like those found in your brain. This is where the liver comes in by providing ketone bodies as an alternative.

Even with this source of energy being available, the body stays in a fasted state as long as there's no food introduced to your digestive system. This causes the ketone bodies to increase in your bloodstream. This increase causes signaling molecules to prompt your cells to start a new state known as autophagy.

Autophagy Explained

To understand autophagy, you must first realize that your body's cells experience wear and tear just like any other part of your body. This could be in the form of worn out organelles, damaged proteins, and damaged membranes. Also, toxins and oxidized particles are created due to the processes inside your cells and the substances and conditions that your body encounters. Although your cells and your body can deal with these in the short term, it can be harmful over time, since it will eventually accumulate and cause disruptions in the cell. Moreover, having this would limit the capabilities of the cells to handle biological stresses. Because of the potential harm present, the cells undergo a process known as autophagy to eliminate the organelles, toxins, free radicals, and damaged proteins in it.

The word autophagy literally means the process of eating itself. This eating of "self" is how the cells solve their trash problem. They will break down the by-products, toxins, and damaged parts into molecules that the cell can use. These can be used as a source of energy to fuel the cell or as raw material to create new and fully functioning organelles to replace old and broken ones. As a result, the cell gets a cleaner and fully functioning system that helps return itself to full efficiency while preventing the harm caused by the accumulation of its trash.

The Different Ways Autophagy Can Start

There are two ways cells can start the process of autophagy. The first is when the cell detects it needs to clean up toxins, by-products, damaged organelles and proteins, and other sub-cellular debris in it. The second is when the cell detects a condition outside of it. These conditions can be divided into two categories: when the cell detects a declining level of blood sugar, and when stressors from the environment are detected. It is under the second way that we can consciously create the conditions required for autophagy. Here are the ways that you can trigger it in your body.

1. Lower blood sugar

As previously mentioned, the body's preferred source of energy is the glucose (or blood sugar) it gets from your diet. This is due to three characteristics of glucose. First, glucose is easily converted from the carbohydrates found in what you eat. Second, your body can easily store excess amounts into fat cells and convert it back if it needs it. Third, the body requires the least amount of input in converting blood sugar to energy compared to other energy sources.

When this convenient and preferred energy source becomes scarce, the body would start looking for more glucose from its stores. These, in the form of glycogen, are made whenever there's an abundance of it. Glycogen is stored in the muscles and the liver and is broken down back into glucose when the body needs it.

Eventually, this store of glucose would also decline (around 14 to 24 hours of fasting). When this occurs, the body would respond by lowering its levels of insulin hormone. This decrease in insulin causes the increase of a hormone known as glucagon, which would then induce autophagy.

In this kind of autophagy, the body is eating up the damaged organelles, by-products, toxins, and old and damaged cells. It does this since these are easily accessible, so it can quickly provide the fuel the different cells in your body need.

The body goes through this natural process whenever it runs out of blood sugar as an easy energy source. It was how pre-agricultural humans were able to go through their day to hunt or forage for food on an empty stomach. It just seems foreign nowadays since food is so accessible that we can easily have at least three full meals in a day to anticipate our body's needs.

You can replicate what our ancestors went through and lower your blood sugar by restricting certain food types, or by following a schedule of your meals and snacks. Choosing food intake can be done through a low carbohydrate diet, like the keto diet, to restrict your body's source of glucose.

On the other hand, scheduling your food intake is done through fasting, which will help deplete your blood sugar.

2. Exercise

Your body requires a quick replenishment of its cells' energy stores during exercise. The body would adapt to it by switching from metabolizing glucose with oxygen to metabolizing glucose alone for energy. This helps cells get the energy that they need immediately.

The problem with producing energy without the help of oxygen is that it produces more by-products. The body and the cells involved anticipate this by starting autophagy. However, autophagy caused by exercise is only limited to the cells involved in metabolic regulation. These cells are those found in the muscle, liver, adipose, and pancreas tissues (16).

There are also some cells in the brain's cerebral cortex that experience autophagy. Although not directly involved with the metabolic regulation, it has a region known as the motor cortex involved with the planning, control, and execution of the voluntary muscles of your body. The activity occurring during exercise in this region is enough to produce similar increase of the by-products from cellular metabolism.

It is no surprise that research has observed intense exercise is the best way to trigger autophagy (17). This is because of such exercises requiring the body to forego oxygen to produce energy at a faster rate. Furthermore, this level of exercise has the greatest demand for muscle repair and rebuilding afterwards since it demands more strength and power from your muscles.

3. Exposure to Hot and Cold Temperatures

Exposure to hot and cold temperatures can cause stress to your body. This stress is enough to trigger autophagy in the affected cells. However, hot and cold temperatures are not equal when it comes to causing autophagy.

Exposure to heat has a more direct effect on autophagy. High temperatures can cause damage to the membrane, proteins, and organelles of cells where the heat was directed. But, the temperature does not necessarily have to reach levels wherein it could result to burns. Temperatures between 40 to 50 degrees Celsius are enough to trigger autophagy in cells. This temperature is enough to cause damage to cell proteins, which are then eliminated through autophagy (18).

On the other hand, cold exposure is not as direct as heat exposure. Cold exposure does not cause autophagy on the cells where it is applied. Instead, it occurs on the nerves due to how the cold sensation affects nerves to communicate the stimuli to the brain (19).

You can benefit from both types of exposure by switching back and forth between hot and cold exposure. This can be done by having a hot shower for thirty minutes before switching to a cold shower for thirty minutes. Another way to do this instead of a shower is through sauna and an ice bath.

4. Food and Antioxidants

There are substances found in food that can indirectly trigger autophagy in your body's cells. Most of these are antioxidants that help your cells get rid of the toxins and free radicals present in your system. In some cases, timing antioxidant intake during a fast can enhance autophagy.

These antioxidants are all naturally occurring substances in the food that we eat. But, in most cases, it is best to obtain it from a supplement since those found in food usually do not have enough to cause a significant effect in your body.

How to Know if Your Body Is in Autophagy

There is no way to directly measure the degree of autophagy in the body. The latest studies have only measured it through human and animal cell culture, and tissue biopsy on animal test subjects. This method would be completely impractical due to its invasive nature.

However, there is a way to gauge it indirectly. The amount of glucose, glucagon, insulin, and ketone bodies found in the blood can indicate the state of the body's metabolism.

Foods, Antioxidants, and Supplements That Promote Autophagy

1. Coconut oil

Coconut oil contains medium chain triglycerides (MCT). These fatty acid helps improve your insulin sensitivity (20). An improved insulin sensitivity can help your body shift faster into autophagy. This is due to the increased sensitivity, helping your body improve how it regulates its insulin levels. It can result to your body requiring lower insulin levels to regulate blood sugar levels. With less insulin circulating in your system, it requires less time to reach the point for autophagy to start.

You can take two tablespoons of coconut oil during your fast or before breaking it. If you do not like its taste, you can buy pure medium chain triglycerides that have been isolated from coconut oil.

2. Vitamin D

Vitamin D decreases the expression of mTOR proteins in your body (21) which triggers the start of autophagy in cells. Also, the introduction of this vitamin to cells promote the death of cancer cells, and the clean-up of harmful bacteria found in cellular organelles.

You can get Vitamin D just by going out and getting some sun. This approach works best during spring or summer. You can also take Vitamin D supplements. You can improve your body's absorption of Vitamin D by taking Vitamin K2 as well.

3. Lithium

Lithium is an essential mineral that triggers autophagy in brain cells. This clean-up process is boosted even further when it comes to breaking down proteins that contribute to psychiatric and neurodegenerative diseases (22). In greater doses, it is taken as medication to manage the symptoms of bipolar personality disorder.

4. Berberine

Berberine is a plant alkaloid that has antidepressant, anti-inflammatory, and neuroprotective effects. It does this by inducing autophagy in the brain cells. This plant alkaloid triggers autophagy indirectly by activating the body's AMPK pathway (23). The activation of this pathway also improves insulin sensitivity and triggers fat metabolism.

Berberine works well with medications taken for diabetes. However, proper care should be done if you are taking anticoagulants and other blood pressure medications since it can also lower blood pressure by thinning your blood.

5. Nicotinamide

Nicotinamide, or niacinamide, is a form of Vitamin B3. It can trigger an autophagy that improves the quality of the mitochondria in human cells (24). This improved quality translates to more efficient energy production and a longer replicative lifespan. A cell that has a longer replicative lifespan means that it can have more generations of newer cells before it loses its ability to reproduce.

6. Acetyl-L-Carnitine

Acetyle-L-Carnitine is the amino acid carnitine's acetylated form. It induces autophagy in the brain cells that helps reverse functional decline and increases protection from oxidative damage. Supplementation with this particular form of the amino acid has been observed to lessen the effects brought about by chronic fatigue, effect improvements on the mood, increase alertness, and cause improvements in mental cognition. [25] [26]

7. Omega-3 fatty acid

This fatty acid has a significant anti-inflammatory effect on our nerves and brain cells. It can help you feel fuller by reducing your hunger and appetite. This effect has been observed in people who consumed fewer calories than their usual meals. Moreover, obese individuals experience a greater effect from the fatty acid's appetite suppression (27).

Also, it has been observed to cause autophagy and increase BDNF signaling in our brain. This results in observed effects such as improved cognition, memory, and mood (28). It also decreases the risk for degenerative diseases of the brain such as Alzheimer's disease, dementia, and mild cognitive impairment. Omega-3 fatty acid can also induce autophagy in the cells of the pancreas, prostate, and cell death in tumors.

Omega-3 fatty acids are fatty acids that your body cannot produce. It must acquire them from dietary sources like sardines, herring, black cod, and salmon. The most convenient way to get your Omega-3 fix is from a supplement like fish oil or krill oil. Just make sure that it is sourced responsibly, and distilled to remove heavy metals and other toxins.

8. Berries

Acai berries, blueberries, and strawberries contain polyphenolic compounds that can activate autophagy in human cells (29). The activation of autophagy is derived from the complete inhibition of proteins that prevent its activation. Direct supplementation of these polyphenols have resulted in reduced oxidative stress and inflammation markers. These also have improved the elimination of toxic proteins present in the cells prior to supplementation.

9. Epigallocatechin gallate

Epigallocatechin gallate or EGCG is a type of plant compound known as cathechin. This compound is found in high amounts in green, white, black, and oolong tea. It is also found in apples, peaches, avocados, pecans, hazelnuts, and pistachios. Out of all of these sources, the best source seems to be green tea due to the concentration of the compound found in it.

EGCG causes autophagy that has a specific anti-inflammatory action (30). It does this by activating the mechanism found in cells that fight inflammation. This same mechanism also protects the cell from the toxic effects of high lipid concentration, and promotes the cell's survivability against toxins and oxidative stress.

10. Ginkgo biloba

Ginkgo biloba induces autophagy by targeting the mTOR signaling pathways. The results brought about by its autophagic effect include decreased cell death caused by stress, a protective effect on cells making up the blood vessels, and reduced inflammation. Furthermore, gingko biloba is able to decrease the damage brought about by diabetic atherosclerosis on the blood vessels (31).

11. Curcumin

Curcumin is the plant compound that gives turmeric its characteristic yellow color. It triggers autophagy in the cells by inhibiting the activation of the mTOR pathway by causing moderate oxidative stress. The autophagy brought about by curcumin has been observed to halt the growth and replication, and to induce the death of pancreatic cancer cells (32). The same effect has been observed on other cancer cells while leaving healthy cells untouched (33).

12. Black Coffee

Coffee without any dairy, cream, sweetener, or sugar can help your cells induce autophagy while fasting (34). This effect is derived from the polyphenols present in coffee. This boost in autophagy has been observed in liver, muscle, and heart cells. The effect lasts one to four hours after drinking black coffee.

However, there are people who do not respond well to coffee. This response will often be stronger during a fast. If you feel anxious or irritated after drinking coffee, you are among the third that should not be drinking coffee while in a fast. This is often due to a sensitivity to caffeine that often precedes an increase in cravings and hunger. Having these sensations would not help and could make you prematurely break your fast.

You can try decaffeinated coffee and see if it does not come with these undesirable effects. Since the autophagy inducing effects of coffee is derived from its polyphenols, you can still benefit from it even with most of the caffeine removed during the roasting process. Just make sure that you are drinking freshly brewed coffee and not one that you made from instant coffee powder. A freshly made brew contains the most number of polyphenols since the manufacturing process to create the instant variant often destroys these beneficial compounds.

13. Caffeine

Caffeine causes autophagy by stimulating the AMP-activated protein kinase (AMPK) pathway of cells found in the body's skeletal muscles (35). This action of caffeine on the muscles is believed to be how it improves muscle activation time and muscular endurance.

14.Resveratrol

Resveratrol is an antioxidant compound found in dark chocolate, grapes, raspberries, and red wine. It induces autophagy in the brain. After inducing autophagy, it resulted in neuroprotective effects in healthy brain cells and accelerated recovery in injured ones.

Moreover, it helps the body improve its insulin sensitivity. This resistance has been observed even among those who consume a diet high in calories. It has even been observed to prevent the development of immature fat cells and growth of existing ones.

Although you can get this antioxidant from food, it is best to find a good supplement for it. The resveratrol content found in food is not enough for your body to reap its benefits.

15.Reishi mushroom

Also known as Ganoderma lucidum, it is a fungus that contains hundreds of bioactive compounds. It is a popular herb in traditional Chinese medicine used for supporting the immune system health, regulating inflammation, alleviating anxiety, and boosting brain function. According to research, its use in Chinese culture is justified due to how it can induce and regulate autophagy in the brain (36).

16.Ginger

Ginger contains an active compound known as 6-shagol. This compound inhibits the activity of mTOR pathways that regulate autophagy (37). 6-shagol triggers cell death in old and malfunctioning cells so that its components can be reused as energy for fueling the metabolism or as raw materials to build healthy cells.

However, this effect is unique to lung cancer cells. Despite this limited effect, it shows a promising potential as a supplement for limiting or stopping the progression of lung cancer during its initial stages.

17. Oleuropein

Oleuropein is a polyphenol found in olive oil that triggers autophagy (38). Because of this, it has potential in preventing or managing Alzheimer's disease and cognitive impairment. Aside from triggering autophagy, it improves the likelihood for cells to undergo autophagy by repairing the organelles in cells that play a role in its activation. The best source of this polyphenol is extra virgin olive oil, olive leaf extract, and argon oil.

18. Sulforaphane

Sulforaphane is a compound found in broccoli, Brussels sprouts, and other cruciferous vegetables. It causes autophagy by inhibiting proteins that lead to its regulation and suppression. The clean-up occurring within the cells goes beyond breaking down damaged proteins, old organelles, and toxins. It has also been credited to the cellular destruction of cells found in colon cancer (39) and breast cancer tumors (40).

19.Galangal

The galangal is a ginger variant native to Thailand. It has a very similar look to ginger but has a sharp and crisp scent similar to citrus fruits. It contains a compound known as galangin that can induce autophagy (41). It has a high anti-tumor activity characterized by halting the cell cycle, promoting cell death and destruction, and reducing the proliferation of cancer cells.

The Progression of Autophagy

Usually, autophagy starts 18 hours into a fasting phase. This is when the ketone bodies reach amounts of around 0.6 to 1.0 mmol/l in the blood. The cells respond to this by releasing the signaling molecules that prompt itself to reduce inflammation and repair damaged DNA.

At the 24-hour mark, the cells start to break down its old and damage components, and unused proteins. When these are broken down, these are used as raw materials to create new components as replacements. In the case of proteins, the resulting amino acids can be used as raw materials or as fuel after being converted to glucose. (42).

Intermittent fasters reach the maximum benefit from autophagy at this point. This is due to the maximum fasting phase having a duration of 24 hours in an intermittent fast.

WARNING: People new to intermittent fasting are highly advised not to do a fast that lasts for more than 24 hours. These fasting phases are beyond what one could consider as intermittent fasting. Those that go through with it undergo a screening and preparation process facilitated by their doctor to avoid any complications. Qualified medical professionals often monitor them throughout the duration of their fast, and provide emergency healthcare if necessary.

From the 48th to the 54th hour of the fasting phase, your body's growth hormone levels average up to five times the normal amount (43). It is also at this stage that your insulin levels decline to their lowest point. This causes a complete stop to the signaling pathways that involve mTOR and insulin. Also, with the absence of insulin in your system, the body gains a relative increase to its insulin sensitivity (44).

Upon reaching 72 hours of fasting, insulin-like growth factor 1 (IGF-1) starts to decrease. IGF-1 promotes the growth in every cell in the body. This decrease would eventually lead to a complete stop to cell growth. These cells would then start to breakdown and recycle old and damaged cells, and damaged and dysfunctional proteins in them. It is also at this point that stem cells increase their stress resistance and regenerative capacity (45).

It should be noted that autophagy can occur at a faster rate. It would depend on how well your body can shift into a fat-burning state. A faster shift would require your body a shorter amount of time during a fasting phase for the ketone bodies to build up and for your cells to shift into autophagy. Because of this, your body might be able to achieve the full effects of autophagy with only 24 hours of fasting through intermittent fasting in the long-term.

How the Body Shifts Back from Autophagy

Like anything that occurs in the body, there is such a thing as too much and too little autophagy. This is why autophagy starts and stops with minimal input from the body. For one induced by low blood sugar through fasting or a ketogenic diet, autophagy immediately ends when the body detects any increase of glucose in your blood. This could be as little as 50 calories from carbohydrates or from protein containing the amino acid leucine.

For intermittent fasting, these calories are introduced during the first meal of your eating phase. Where you get these first few calories is important if you want to maximize the clean-up that your body experiences during autophagy. It should come from a balanced and nutritious meal that contains a substantial amount of vegetables, plant fats, and plant fiber. Protein should come from lean cuts of meat while carbohydrates should come from whole sources and legumes.

Benefits of Intermittent Fasting

You have read what happens in your body when you do intermittent fasting. You have also read how it influences certain hormones, and how it affects certain organs and systems. In this chapter, you will have a closer look on how exactly intermittent fasting causes these changes. You will learn why these changes are important for your goal of losing weight and your overall health.

Weight Loss

To lose weight, you have to consume consistently fewer calories than how much your body needs. This lower calorie consumption results in a calorie deficit that forces your body to turn to an energy source other than glucose. At first, it will burn glycogen. When this runs out, it will start burning the body fat that we are aiming to lose.

The common approach to induce a caloric deficit is by following a calorie-restricted diet. However, this would require you the tedious work of counting the calories of your every meal, which is impractical, especially if you are eating out. And, with our caloric requirements varying for every single day, your calorie deficit would rarely be consistent.

This is where intermittent fasting can make weight loss easier for you. All you would have to do is follow a schedule for when you can and cannot eat. This would naturally make you lose some meals for the day, which puts your body at a calorie deficit.

Out of the two methods, intermittent fasting is easier to do. And, with one study stating that both methods can provide similar weight loss results (46), you are basically getting the same benefit for less work with intermittent fasting.

However, fasting provides even more weight loss benefits than simple fat loss. Intermittent fasting also increases the insulin sensitivity, human growth hormone production in your body. These help your body even further in losing unwanted weight from body fat. Here's how these help you in achieving weight loss:

1. Less body fat stored

Every fasting phase while intermittently fasting depletes the glucose present in your blood and the glycogen stored in your muscles. This helps the body get used to requiring less than its usual insulin levels to respond to increased blood sugar levels. This decreased requirement for insulin means that the body has regained its sensitivity for the hormone (47).

The increased insulin sensitivity makes the body more efficient in using glucose for energy. With less insulin going around, your blood sugar goes to where it is needed. It would not go to your body fat cells, which will make you regain the weight you lose while fasting or exercising.

2. Better muscle growth

Fasting increases your body's production of human growth hormone. By itself, an increased production of this hormone does not have any effect on weight loss. But, when it's combined with calorie restriction, a higher production of human growth hormone can accelerate weight loss by helping you burn fat (48). The increase in fat burning occurs due to human growth hormone increasing the breakdown and use of fat for fueling the body's metabolism.

Do not worry about looking bulky. Women naturally have lower testosterone levels. Because of this, your muscles do not grow in the same way or rate as men. Of course, there are women that choose to bulk up in such a way. However, these are often achieved with external intervention to boost testosterone production.

3. Maintain lean muscle mass

The problem with most weight loss and fat loss diets is that losing weight comes with losing muscle mass. Losing your muscle mass is the last thing you want when losing weight. It decreases how much calories your body needs on a daily basis. With reduced calorie needs, your body would eventually reach a caloric surplus even if you maintain your caloric intake. This risk of caloric surplus becomes even greater once you achieved your weight loss goal and stop restricting your diet. Either way, you would eventually gain the fat that you lost.

In intermittent fasting, this rebound is not likely to happen since it can preserve your lean muscle mass even when the body is deficient of calories. One study has observed that intermittent fasting can maintain lean muscle mass while promoting fat loss among obese individuals (49). This helps your body maintain its metabolism while getting rid of unwanted body fat. Because of this, you would not reach a caloric surplus even as long as you maintain your caloric intake.

Maintaining this lean muscle mass is crucial if you aim to have a defined figure when you finally shed the unwanted body fat from your physique. Doing intermittent fasting instead of focusing on restricting calories for weight loss will help you avoid getting the flat muscle look most women get that result from such diets. Of course, maintaining this definition when you achieve your intended fat loss requires that you already have created a foundation of muscle mass for it or working towards it. If you are working towards it while intermittently fasting, you would have to do resistance training.

4. Improves keto-adaptation

Our bodies normally use both glucose and fat as energy sources. However, due to a diet of high carbohydrates being the norm, we lost the ability to easily switch between using glucose and fat for fueling our metabolism.

Intermittent fasting helps you regain this ability by frequently depleting your body's glucose and stored glycogen. Once this is depleted, the body has no choice but to resort to a fat burning state. Eventually, the body will have an easier time to keto-adapt, which is its ability to switch from glucose to fat for energy.

Better keto-adaptation gives you more stable energy levels so you would have less cravings for food. Also, since your body switches to using fat more quickly, you are burning fat even when the body is only at standing or sitting down (50).

5. Decreased food cravings

Normally, when you think that you're hungry, you are actually just craving for food. These instances of food craving are brought about by the rapid or prolonged increase of your insulin levels. Intermittent fasting helps your body learn what it actually means to be hungry by helping it regain its insulin sensitivity (51). Once it reaches healthy levels of insulin sensitivity, the body stops producing more insulin than it actually needs. As a result, you are less likely to have sugar cravings despite having normal blood sugar levels.

Intermittent fasting also decreases food cravings and increases your tolerance against hunger (52). It also improves the response of the body when releasing the hormone inducing the sensation of fullness and satiety. As a result, one is less likely to overeat since they can immediately feel when they have eaten enough.

This greatly benefits women doing an intermittent fast. This is due to women being more likely to experience food cravings on a daily basis (53). To make it worse, food cravings experienced by women are for sweet foods like pastries, chocolate, and ice cream. The increased insulin sensitivity, improved hunger tolerance, and more responsive satiety can help manage these cravings, especially during the culmination of your monthly menstrual cycle when these cravings are at their strongest.

6. More manageable appetite

Intermittent fasting lowers your appetite. This results to you eating less and helping you maintain or lose weight. This decreased appetite arises from the effect of intermittent fasting on the hormones that regulate your hunger and satiety.

The body decreases its production of leptin and ghrelin after going through a schedule of intermittent fasting (54). This helps you have more manageable meals than a simple calorie restricted diet. You are essentially eating less since you do not feel like eating more and already feel satisfied with what you ate.

Promotes muscle gain and fat loss at the same time

An intermittent fasting regimen provides the best conditions to make it possible for you to gain muscle and lose fat at the same time. Training during the fasting phase helps your body to use more of its fat stores for energy. Then, when you break your fast after your workout, your body gets the nutrients it needs for recovery and building new muscle proteins. This was what has been observed in a study involving recreationally active individuals following an eight-week schedule of intermittent fasting and resistance training (55).

Furthermore, intermittent fasting increases your body's production of human growth hormone. Human growth hormone stimulates the various tissues in your body to release IGF-1. IGF-1 promotes amino acid uptake and its synthesis of muscle fibers (56). As a result, your body gets to recover and adapt to the stresses placed upon it by your workout.

It should be noted that the benefit of losing fat while gaining muscle requires more than following an intermittent fasting regimen. The same rules still apply when it comes to gaining muscle: you need to progressively train your strength and have a diet that supports its growth. You would also have to be smart about your choices for carbohydrates and caloric intake if you also want to lose fat.

Improved recovery from workout

Due to increased insulin sensitivity, your body is more efficient in allocating glucose to where it is needed. This means your muscles get the energy needed to recover from your workout. This energy can be used in helping the muscles recover and grow new muscle proteins.

However, it should be noted that muscle gain can suffer if the body is not getting what it needs from its diet. You have to consume enough calories to provide the energy needed to build muscles. You should also consume enough branch chain amino acids so your body has the necessary building blocks for muscle growth.

Also, with fasting inducing autophagy, your body becomes better at recovery and building muscle (57). This is due to autophagy improving the efficiency of the cells involved in repairing muscle cells and creating new muscle proteins. The more efficient cells can also help those who experienced muscle damage and trauma since autophagy also improves regeneration of muscle tissues.

An easier method to improve conditions of obesity

Other than problems with a person's genetic make-up, obesity is caused by a lifestyle of low physical activity and high carbohydrate and fat consumption. Those that find themselves in such a situation would usually resort to restricting their calories to lose weight. Unfortunately, most obese individuals often find this approach a drastic approach since the caloric restrictions are far below than what they are used to.

This is where some researchers turned to intermittent fasting as an alternative to help obese women ranging from 35 to 70 years of age. According to the study, intermittent fasting is effective in weight loss even without restricting food intake (58). The weight loss recorded is an average of 5 percent of their starting weight. Furthermore, if combined with a diet restricting food intake to 70 percent, participants lost twice the weight lost by intermittent fasters that have no dietary restrictions.

It should be noted that doing an intermittent fast without restricting the diet is only good for the short term. It can increase one's fasting insulin levels, which can be detrimental to long-term weight loss goals. This approach is useful as a starting point so obese individuals can gradually reduce their food intake.

Reduces visceral fat

Visceral fat is a body fat type found in your abdominal cavity. It can be found near, attached to, or surrounding your stomach, liver, arteries, and intestines. Unlike subcutaneous fat (the one you find under your skin), visceral fat increase your likelihood for serious health disorders like Alzheimer's disease, type 2 diabetes, liver insulin resistance, colorectal cancer, and breast cancer. Also, this fat increases the inflammation in your body, which could promote the accumulation of plaque in the arteries. Eventually, it could lead to a heart attack, ruptured or blocked arteries, and stroke.

Intermittent fasting can reduce the existing visceral fat in your body in two ways. First, it restricts caloric intake by having a limited time for eating. This helps your body burn body fat – both subcutaneous and visceral. Over time, the body metabolizes visceral fat tissue deposits until these are reduced to harmless amounts.

Second, intermittent fasting induces autophagy in the body. The body's self-eating mechanism protects the body from the formation of these harmful fat deposits (59). This helps manage and prevent new visceral fat deposits from forming as you are losing the existing ones. As for the existing fat deposits, autophagy increases the rate the body metabolizes visceral fat tissue into energy (60).

Lower risk for Type 2 Diabetes

Type 2 diabetes is a complication brought about by chronically elevated insulin levels. This causes the body to resist the effects of the hormone. With glucose unregulated, it can easily accumulate in your bloodstream. At its initial stages, the symptoms include increased hunger and thirst, frequent urination, sugar in the urine, blurred vision, and headache. In the long term, it could lead to complications in the cardiovascular system, nervous system, kidneys, eyes, bones, and joints.

Intermittent fasting helps to manage the blood sugar levels by restricting food intake at a set timeframe. The body does not get a new supply of blood sugar while it is restricted from eating. This forces the body to use up the glucose available in its bloodstream. This causes a decline in blood sugar levels. The body detects this decrease and lowers the insulin in its bloodstream.

Furthermore, there is an increase in insulin sensitivity every time a fast ends due to the release of glucagon-like peptide 1 (GLP1). This increased insulin sensitivity frequently occurs with intermittent fasting. In the long run, the body returns its insulin sensitivity to healthy levels.

Aside from this, intermittent fasting improves the overall function of the pancreas. Poor pancreas function is one of the factors believed to worsen conditions of type 2 diabetes (61). This reduced function is caused by pancreatic fat, malfunctioning pancreatic beta cells, or both. With intermittent fasting, these fat deposits in the pancreas are metabolized by the body for energy.

And, with a fast-induced autophagy, the dysfunctional and damaged organelles in the pancreas are broken down into reusable components. These are then used to build new organelles that let the pancreatic cells secrete insulin into the bloodstream (62).

Alternate day fasting is the method that works best to lower the risk of type 2 diabetes and improve pancreas function. This method was what research has observed to be effective. In this particular regimen, those that experienced improvement followed a 75 percent energy restriction during their fasting days (63).

Maintains and enhances brain health

7. Anti-aging benefits

As you age, the nerve cells of your brain go through natural changes. These are evidenced by slower reflexes, increasing difficulty in memory recall, reduced cognition, and slower decision-making as we grow old. Unfortunately, aging can be accelerated by the oxidative stress, toxic exposure, and amyloid beta-accumulation on our brain and its cells.

Intermittent fasting can help slow down these effects caused by aging. In some cases, these effects are even completely reversed. This anti-aging effect arises from the use of ketone bodies as an energy source while the body is under a fasting phase.

The use of ketone bodies causes neurons in your brain's hippocampus to produce more mitochondria for energy production that increases the efficiency of each cell in doing its job.

It increases the expression of the BDNF protein. This results in the inhibition of brain cell death, which helps preserve old brain cells so it can be repaired or reused by the body through autophagy. It also boosts the adaptability of the synapses of brain cells, which helps in its ability to change and adapt to the new information our brain receives or transmits.

Ketone bodies also prevent the production of free radicals in neurons. This is due to free radicals being a by-product of glucose metabolism. In addition to this, ketones stimulate the antioxidant activity present in neurons.

Aside from introducing ketone bodies to the brain, the repeated switching between fat and glucose metabolism boosts the resilience of your brain's cells and its neuronal circuits (64). The shifting strengthens the stress resistance of activated brain cells and increases the preparedness of these cells to transmit signals through the nervous system. This effect seems to be caused by the molecular recycling and pathway repair occurring in the cell due to the autophagy induced by fasting. This is combined with the creation of new neurons, synapses, and mitochondria when the body shifts into growth upon breaking the fast. Due to the nature of intermittent fasting, these two phases occur repeatedly in a cycle. This translates to a compounding effect of increasing efficiency for the existing cells and promoting cell, synapse, and mitochondria growth.

Lastly, when breaking a fast, the body releases the hormone glucagon-like peptide 1 (GLP1). The GLP1 hormone promotes insulin release from the pancreas and increases the insulin sensitivity of various cells. It does this by interacting with the neurons found in your spinal cord and those that connect it to your different organs. This interaction has an added effect of improving the signal cognition, stress resistance, and synaptic plasticity of these nerves (65). This results in the nerves being more efficient in transmitting signals between your brain and the various organs found in your cardiovascular system and digestive system. Moreover, since it can cross the blood-brain barrier, these benefits are also felt by your brain cells.

8. Reduces the occurrence of epileptic seizures

Epilepsy is a disorder of the central nervous system. It causes abnormal brain activity that triggers seizures, episodes of unusual behavior, weird sensations, and loss of awareness. The seizures that occur are the distinguishing symptom of epilepsy. This could be in the form of a blank stare that lasts for a few seconds or in the form of repeatedly twitching limbs.

Half of those with epilepsy cannot be determined as to what caused it to occur in the first place. For others, their condition has been attributed to their genes, to a traumatic injury on the head, to brain tumors and strokes, to infectious diseases, to developmental disorders, and to prenatal injury.

Treatment is limited to the management of its symptoms, particularly the seizures. However, the medication used to manage epileptic seizures only work for two out of every three patients.

An alternative treatment to anti-seizure medication is intermittent fasting. It turns out intermittent fasting helps reduce the occurrence of epileptic seizures through a neuroprotective effect (66). This has been observed among patients that followed a modified 5/2 method wherein they can only eat two meals on two days every week. But, there's a greater decrease in seizure frequency for those that fasted for 24 hours once a month.

As you might have noticed, the fasting method done by the patients are not as restrictive as what a normal 5/2 method or eat-stop-eat method would entail. This is due to these patients are all below the age of 10. They cannot fast as adults can or else they can experience complications that can affect their growth. If you plan to use intermittent fasting to manage epileptic seizures, you might be able to do a fasting schedule that stays true to the mentioned methods. Keep in mind that you should still consult your doctor before doing so in order to ensure your safety and long-term health.

9. Assist in the treatment and recovery from brain damage

Brain damage is any kind of injury that results in the destruction or weakening of your brain cells. It is not a degenerative disease or a congenital defect caused by birth trauma or genetics. Furthermore, the damage it causes is confined to a local area. This remains the same even in cases of closed head injuries wherein the damage is diffused to multiple areas of the brain.

Brain damage can be divided into two categories – acquired and traumatic. Both of these have similar symptoms that vary depending on the severity of the injury. Mild injuries are temporary and do not cause noticeable symptoms. Moderate ones lasts for a longer time and cause symptoms that are more noticeable. Serious brain damage can cause debilitating and permanent conditions.

Traumatic Brain Injury

Traumatic brain injury is damage resulting from an external force. This external force can be caused by falls, physical assault, sports injuries, and accidents. The primary damage caused by these events cause secondary brain damage attributed to increased inflammation, high oxidative stress, and brain cell death. Physical, speech, and occupational therapy rarely addresses these aspects of traumatic brain injury due to brain cells having a different mechanism for recovery. Fortunately, intermittent fasting has been found to have a positive effect on these conditions.

This effect from intermittent fasting is attributed to autophagy (67). It provides the brain protection from oxidative stress and inflammation. At the same time, it prevents cell death by replacing old and damaged parts, or by breaking down harmful substances that built up due to the injury. If this is not possible, the body recycles the components of damaged cells to create new ones.

Using intermittent fasting to help recovery from traumatic brain injury is only limited to moderate damage. Furthermore, the benefits have only been observed if the fast only lasts up to 24 hours (68).

Acquired Brain Injury

This type of brain injury is acquired through the lack of oxygen caused by drowning, strangulation, stroke, aneurysm, tumor growth, or a heart attack. These causes the brain cells to lose access to oxygen that arises from the body not being able to breathe air or having its blood flow cut off from a part of the brain.

Intermittent fasting through an alternate day fasting schedule can improve conditions of acquired brain injury through autophagy (69). This was what had been observed from test subjects that had experienced a stroke or a heart attack. The brain cells that lost access to healthy blood flow displayed reduced tissue damage and increased functionality. It shows that brain cells can be repaired and help patients to regain, at least, a part of their brain function after experiencing blood and oxygen deprivation.

As for brain tumors, a fast-induced autophagy can help manage during the early phases. Tumor growth is suppressed due to the cleanup of damaged organelles and recycling of molecules in the brain cells. However, it can make the condition worse in the later stages by promoting the survivability of cancer cells (70).

10. Decrease risk for degenerative disorders of the brain

As it ages, brain cells accumulate a formation of proteins inside. Although it is not clear what purpose this protein has, protein accumulation in brain cells disrupt its overall efficiency. This loss in efficiency is characterized by the poor transmission between neurons, decreased organelle function, and weaker synapse between multiple brain cells. Eventually, if the protein accumulation does not stop, it could eventually lead to a neurodegenerative disorder like dementia, Parkinson's, and Alzheimer's disease (71).

Intermittent fasting can help manage or stop the progression of such disorders by increasing the production of the BDNF protein in nerve cells. BDNF, or brain-derived neurotrophic factor, helps support the learning, processing, and memory function of your brain. It increases the stress resistance and survivability of the nerve cells. And, more importantly, it promotes the production of new nerve cells in the brain.

Aside from this, the autophagy induced by intermittent fasting improves the efficiency of the brain cells. It does this by breaking down the protein that have been building up into amino acids, which are used to grow new cells or organelles. Moreover, damaged and dysfunctional cellular components are broken down and reused for creating new ones. This results to brain cells working better than it previously did (72).

The ketone bodies produced by the liver while on a fasted state also improve markers indicating neurodegenerative disease (73). These particular markers are the accumulation of neuron plaque and neurofibrillary tangles, both of which contribute to Alzheimer's and Parkinson's disease. Furthermore, cognition improved among those that showed brain function deterioration while fasting or after consuming medium chain triglycerides.

Increased cellular repair

Intermittent fasting increases the production of human growth hormone in the body. This hormone activates the Foxm1b gene in various cells, which triggers responsible for healing and regeneration. The importance of this gene in our bodies is evident with how tissue repair becomes impaired as the levels of human growth hormone decline as we age. To confirm this, one study inserted Foxm1b gene into old animal test subjects. The study observed tissue regeneration similar to the rate observed in younger test subjects (74).

This same effect has been observed in humans. Human growth hormone was able to promote kidney growth in patients with chronic kidney failure. Although it is still being testing, it shows potential for addressing problems involving organ failure caused by a chronic condition (75).

Cellular repair is also enhanced thanks to autophagy. This is an expected benefit since autophagy is essentially the mechanism of our cells to repair itself and its organelles. It was already mentioned that it can repair and revive damage neurons in the brain. But, autophagy is more than just a measure in preventing neurodegeneration. It also repairs the cells found in your liver and heart, which are both incapable of self-regeneration without the assistance of autophagy.

It also repairs the cells found in your bones and joints. It is believed that increasing autophagy on older individuals can prevent the degeneration of your bones and joints, which eventually leads to osteoarthritis (76). Moreover, this repairing actions was also observed in tissues that are already degenerating. Because of this, some medical researchers suggest that that it has a therapeutic potential for treating osteoporosis and other bone diseases (77).

Overall anti-aging protection

Intermittent fasting increases the lifespan and oxidative protection of your cells (78). The increased resilience results from the manageable stress placed on the body by intermittent fasting. This process is known as hormesis. To illustrate, think of it as your cells lifting weight through intermittent fasting so it can lift the weight of actual oxidative stress.

The same increase in cellular longevity has been observed in cells after undergoing autophagy (79). It does this by replacing old and damage cellular parts by breaking them down and using the materials to build new ones or repair what can be repaired. This cleanup and repair inside the cell fixes age-related defects in the tissues and organs of the body and rejuvenate the cell as a whole.

Increased energy

Intermittent fasting can help your body acclimate to using body fat as a fuel. When you achieve this, your body has an easier time metabolizing nutrients for its energy needs. This is due to fat and ketone bodies only requiring three steps for the body to use it as fuel. This is in contrast to glucose needing 11 steps before it can provide energy to the body (80). This results in a greater endurance before feeling exhausted in doing high-intensity exercises and lasting longer in steady-state cardio exercises.

This increased energy also benefits your day-to-day life. With your body having adapted to easily switch between glucose and fat burning as needed, you would rarely, if not never, feel low on energy when your blood sugar drops. This is due to your body having a ready supply of fat that it can easily use as a fuel source.

Improved cardiovascular health

1. Manage high blood pressure

High blood pressure, otherwise known as hypertension, is a condition that develops gradually for most people. If left untreated, it can lead to complications such as loss or degradation of eyesight, stroke, heart failure, and kidney disease. There are a variety of health conditions that can lead to it. The most common include obesity, high cholesterol, and type 2 diabetes.

Intermittent fasting can lower blood pressure as confirmed by a study done on humans. It involved more than a thousand individuals that followed a fasting schedule for 21 days (81). The observation was that the improvement in blood pressure can be attributed to the increase in insulin sensitivity, increased activity of BDNF, and higher norepinephrine production. Unfortunately, blood pressure returned to its hypertensive levels once the study participants finished their 21-day intermittent fasting schedule. However, a similar study that went for five weeks observed a more permanent improvement (82). This shows that intermittent fasting requires a longer timeframe for results to remain once you stop fasting.

For women, it is important to have a proactive approach in managing blood pressure. This is due to the risk of developing it increases dramatically once you reach around 55 to 65 years of age. It is also best to avoid lifestyle choices that contribute to hypertension like smoking, a sedentary lifestyle, and a high sodium diet.

2. Lower blood cholesterol

High blood cholesterol is the condition wherein the blood contains unhealthy levels of bad (LDL) cholesterol. This can be caused by type 2 diabetes upsetting the balance between LDL and HDL cholesterol, high blood sugar levels, high carbohydrate diet, and oxidative stress. Having this condition increases your risk for a stroke, coronary heart disease, atherosclerosis, and peripheral vascular disease due to its tendency to cause plaque buildup along the arteries. Hypertension often comes together with this condition due to cholesterol buildup causing blockages or narrowing of blood vessels and hardened arteries.

Intermittent fasting helps improve high blood cholesterol by improving the balance between the good and bad cholesterol (83). It does this by increasing HDL levels while reducing total cholesterol levels in your blood. Furthermore, the body's state of ketosis shifts the body's metabolism into fat burning mode and looks for fat that can be used for energy. Visceral fat is among the fat stores targeted to fuel the body's energy requirements. This particular body fat increases LDL concentration in the blood by increasing VLDL particle concentration and insulin resistance (84). With it reduced to a certain level, this increased production of LDL cholesterol stops.

While the body is in a fat burning state, LDL cholesterol levels and total cholesterol balance is improved even further. One of the ketone bodies produced by the body can trigger the liver's niacin receptors. When this is triggered, the liver stops synthesizing LDL cholesterol while maintaining the one for HDL cholesterol (85).

It should be noted that intermittent fasting should only be done on the short term if you have high blood cholesterol. Doing it in the short term can improve LDL levels but long term intermittent fasting can increase bad cholesterol levels again. Also, it is also best to consume a healthy and well-balanced diet while doing an intermittent fast and to just stick to the 16/8 method. This helps in minimizing the risk of high blood cholesterol as observed in those following the alternate day fasting method.

3. Reduce arterial plaque

The formation of plaque on your arteries leads to a condition known as atherosclerosis. Other than cholesterol, these deposits contain fibrin, calcium, cell waste products, and fatty substances. The specific location of plaque would vary from one person to another. Because of this, atherosclerosis does not always cause the same complications. Conditions usually caused by plaque formation include coronary heart disease, carotid artery disease, angina, peripheral artery disease, and chronic kidney disease.

Aside from decreasing blood flow to heart muscles or the kidney, atherosclerotic plaque deposits can also cause complete blockages in an artery. This can be by a broken off plaque deposit that got stuck in a blood vessel, or a blood clot forming between a narrow channel between the plaque and the blood vessel's wall. If this blockage occurs in the brain or heart, the body can experience a heart or a stroke. In other cases, it could block of blood flow to your extremities that can result in tissue death.

Autophagy induced by intermittent fasting can help clear these deposits and reduce the risk of conditions that arise from atherosclerosis (86). Unlike the one that prompts cellular repair, the autophagy that occurs focuses on clearing excess cholesterol and preventing the expansion of these deposits. This is done through the action of fatty acids floating in your bloodstream.

This autophagy on plaque deposits works at a slower rate of breakdown. It provides cell protection on the healthy smooth muscle cells of the artery while breaking down and reconstructing damaged components in these cells. Combined, the plaque deposits remain firmly attached to the arteries and does not have a risk of breaking off.

Better Skin

Your skin quality deteriorates as you age. It incurs UV light damage from its exposure to the sun. It loses fibers known as elastin that help keep your skin's tightness. This results in the skin sagging and wrinkling, pores increasing in size, and skin looking thinner. For some, the skin gets more age spots, moles, freckles, and other skin pigmentations.

Autophagy can help bring back the youthful years to your skin (87). This was observed in one study wherein fasting increased skin stem cells, which could lead to younger looking skin thanks to better quality skin cells. Also, the skin regains its collagen for its youthful glow through the increased turnover of skin cells.

It is not only aging women that can enjoy this benefit brought by autophagy. Women who just gave birth or lost weight can also benefit from it. The stretching of the skin from weight gain or pregnancy would leave them with excess skin cells in the form of stretch marks and loose skin after losing weight or giving birth. Autophagy can fix this by clearing out cells that have no use, like the loose skin or stretch marks. Some people that lost their weight by using intermittent fasting from the very start say that it prevented stretch marks and loose skin.

Manages Type 2 Diabetes

Intermittent fasting forces your body to metabolize all its glucose and glycogen stores during the fasting phase. By using this up, the body returns to a state wherein it can relearn how it feels like to have no sugar in the bloodstream. This helps their cells regain insulin sensitivity little by little. Over time, the body regains a healthy response and stops excessive insulin release to regulate glucose levels.

Because of this effect, it is not surprising that people with type 2 diabetes can improve their condition through intermittent fasting. One study observed this improvement from their participants after 18 days of intermittent fasting through an alternate day fasting plan or a weekly three-day fasting plan (88). Their improvements reached the point wherein they can stop taking insulin and reduce their oral medication for managing type-2 diabetes. They experienced significant loss in terms of body weight, waist circumference, and glycated blood cells. All of these indicate that their blood sugar is properly regulated and that they have a healthy response to insulin.

Intermittent fasting also works for those with obesity-induced type-2 diabetes. Although it works the same as the average diabetes, this is caused by the stresses placed on parts of the cell membrane, which leads to the suppression of insulin receptor signals. Intermittent fasting was able to improve the transmission of insulin receptor signals in these cells. At the same time, it improved the how well the pancreas responds to changes in the blood sugar and tolerates elevated levels of glucose. It does this by improving the survivability, efficiency, oxidative stress tolerance, and regeneration of pancreatic cells (89).

Improved Immune Response

Although autophagy is naturally activates as part of your body's immune response, fasting can still enhance your immunity through a fast-induced autophagy. This improves your immune system's response by making your white blood cells more efficient (90). These cells adapt more quickly, have higher survivability, and have healthier and more efficient organelles. This results in an adaptive immune system that learns faster as it encounters toxins and infectious pathogens, and experiences the stresses placed on the body by itself and its environment. It also improves how well it retains what it learned from these so it can respond more easily when it occurs again in the future.

Furthermore, autophagy eliminates the toxic and infectious substances floating around in your body (91). These are broken into simpler forms and reused for its components for the body's raw material needs. This cleans up the body of harmful substances and infectious organisms that can cause harm to the body if left alone.

Helps prevent and fight cancer

Intermittent fasting can help prevent cancer by improving insulin sensitivity that prevents excessive amounts of the hormone from circulating in your body. Insulin resistance increases your risk for having cancer. In fact, women who are insulin resistant have three times the risk for breast cancer than those who are insulin sensitive (92). This increased risk is also true for cancers of the colon, endometrium (inner lining of the uterus), kidney, liver, ovaries, and pancreas (93). The culprit behind this is the high levels of insulin, which can promote cell growth in your body. Unfortunately, insulin does not discriminate which cells grow and, as a result, it can promote cancer cells to grow.

Moreover, since intermittent fasting induces autophagy, it can also have a more direct influence in preventing cancer. Cancer cells start as normal healthy cells that became defective at some point. Autophagy helps the body remove these cells in your system by breaking them down. In some cases, it can prevent this cellular malfunction from happening in the first place by targeting the defective parts in the cells. It does not even have to destroy these parts since autophagy can also repair a cell organelle if it can still be salvaged (94).

As for fighting cancer with intermittent fasting, it is a possible measure for those that do not suffer from malnutrition or severe weight loss (95). It is effective in preventing growth and reducing the mass of certain tumors. Furthermore, it widens the window available for cancer treatments and helps the body increase its tolerance for chemotherapy. This helps decrease the side effects of the treatment, which makes it possible to decrease antibiotic use and increase the dose or frequency of treatment.

However, proper care and consultation should first before using it as an aid for treating cancer. Intermittent fasting is not recommended as a measure to treat or aid in treating certain types of cancer. Fasting also limits a person's nutrient intake, which is the last thing a cancer patient would need since the body uses micronutrients to fight it and cope with the treatment. Furthermore, the research looking into the viability of short term or long term fasting is still in its infancy. There is still a lack of knowledge what it can do to the body given the different variables that could exist in a person's unique situation.

Decreased Risk for Metabolic Syndrome

Metabolic syndrome is a condition that results from the combination of various health problems. These include high belly fat, high body weight, high blood pressure, high LDL cholesterol, low HDL cholesterol, and high triglycerides. This eventually leads to insulin resistance. Once this happens, it increases the risk for type-2 diabetes together with the already high risk for a heart attack or stroke.

Intermittent fasting is effective in improving metabolic syndrome for the simple reason that it will help in making a person lose fat and in regaining healthy levels of its metabolism. This comes with regaining healthy levels of HDL and LDL cholesterol, blood pressure, and triglycerides. Together with this, the body would also regain its insulin sensitivity that provides great effect in preventing or reducing complications with type-2 diabetes.

Younger Biological Age

Your chronological age is the number of years that you have been alive. But, your chronological age does not indicate how young or old our bodies are. This is where biological age comes in. Unlike your chronological age that stays the same regardless of your choices, it takes into account the impact of various lifestyle choices like your diet, daily exercise and activity level, stress, and medications.

To determine this, tissue samples of a person and the genes found in it are catalogued. What was catalogued would then be compared to a list of 150 genes that give a person their "healthy gene score". Basically, if you get an equivalent gene score expected of your age, you have the health expected for your chronological age. If you get a better score, you are healthier than most of your generation and have a younger biological age. The opposite is the case if you get a lower score, which implies that you are more likely to have a degenerative or chronic disease sooner than those in your chronological age group (96).

Someone's biological age can also be hinted by one's appearance. Although it can be inaccurate, people who look and move younger than their age indicate they have a younger biological age than their chronological age. You would usually notice these in people who consistently exercise and have follow a good sleeping schedule. This is not a coincidence since these two activities can trigger autophagy (97).

Whether through fasting or exercise, putting the body into autophagy helps your cells return to its vitality. It removes any debris inside the cells that may disrupt it from functioning at its best. It basically gets rid of the old and dead, and reuses what it can get from to make things in tip-top shape.

Furthermore, autophagy and fasting improves the function of existing mitochondria and the quality of new ones built later on. This particular organelle is an important indicator for one's biological age since those with stronger mitochondria have been found to live longer (98).

Why Women Should Take Advantage of the Benefits of Intermittent Fasting

Women aged 25 to 34 have an increased risk of gaining weight. This risk is even greater for women who have a history of obesity in their family, who have issues with their hormones, who have post-traumatic stress disorder, and who are taking certain medications. Every woman should consider this risk and take measures to mitigate it. This is due to overweight women being more likely to increase their risk for various health conditions.

Overweight women are at risk for 13 different kinds of cancer. This includes cancer of the breast, endometrial, gallbladder, throat, kidney, thyroid, liver, colon, rectal, meningioma, ovaries, and pancreas. They are also twice as likely to develop type 2 diabetes and metabolic syndrome. They also have poorer cardiovascular health markers that indicate their higher chance for cardiovascular events like a heart attack or a stroke. They will also have more trouble getting pregnant and increase their chances of complications during pregnancy, such as preeclampsia, high blood pressure, and gestational diabetes.

This is where the benefits of intermittent fasting, particularly those on weight-loss, come in. Intermittent fasting can help women lose their weight by triggering the body's fat burning state. The weight lost is also easier to maintain by increasing insulin sensitivity. And, since intermittent fasting does not require the work most diets do, women will have a better chance of success since they are more likely to stick to it.

Intermittent fasting also brings about the body's natural self-cleaning and self-repairing mechanism. This plays a role in reducing the risk of so many degenerative diseases that women are at a much greater risk of acquiring. For example, diseases like Alzheimer's disease, osteoporosis, osteoarthritis, and stroke. In addition to these, there are also diseases unique to women that can lead to fatal consequences such as cancer of the breast, ovaries, and cervix. Through autophagy, the risk for these diseases are dramatically reduced due to its effect on keeping the cells that make up these tissues, organs, and systems in top shape.

As you can see, other than health conditions that could be aggravated, there is no reason why women should not do intermittent fasting. In fact, it should even be encouraged that women attempt should at least try a decent attempt for it for a month or two. Such a short time could already have positive effects on their health. And, by doing so, maybe they can see that it is not such a big deal to start eating your meals at a later time. It cannot even be placed under the same view as the calorie restriction diet, which is often viewed as a short-term punishment for long-term gain. It is a weight loss strategy that is very sustainable given the fact that it can be, and are being, done as a permanent fixture in their lifestyle.

What Women Need to Watch Out For

The physiological differences between men and women results in differences in experience when doing a diet or a workout plan. This is the same case for intermittent fasting. Also, if done in the exact same way as some male fitness experts would suggest, intermittent fasting can result in more harm than good for your body.

So, before getting started, you need to first realize what you might experience from intermittent fasting that is unique to women. There would be things that you should watch out for if you want avoid negative effects on your health. Also, there might be changes that you have to implement so you can avoid these. Such considerations are even more important if one is at risk for a disease, pregnant, breastfeeding, or menopausal. Here are the considerations you must take into account when doing an intermittent fast and some suggestions to avoid or manage these effects.

Negative Effects on Fertility

Men and women have the same glands that regulate the release of their hormones. These glands also release the same hormones – gonadotropin releasing hormone (GnRH), luteinizing hormone (LH), and follicular stimulating hormone (FSH). The difference between men and women is how their reproductive system works.

Men do not follow a schedule when producing testosterone and sperm. On the other hand, although their bodies continuously produce estrogen and progesterone hormones, women go through a cycle before they release mature egg cells and be fertile. This cycle requires precise release of the hormone GnRH. If the timing is interrupted, it will disrupt your reproductive cycle. Unfortunately, GnRH is highly sensitive to changes in the body and the environment. These changes include those that affect your sleep, stress levels, and food and nutritional intake.

Because of this, it is not surprising that some women experience irregular reproductive cycles when they do intermittent fasting. This irregularity often results from at least one of two things – poor protein consumption or elevated stress levels.

Poor protein intake

Low protein intake has this effect on your reproductive cycle due to it providing the amino acids necessary to activate your estrogen receptors. Activation of these receptors result to the liver producing IGF-1, which would trigger the thickening of your uterine wall and the progression of your reproductive cycle.

Elevated stress levels

Intermittent fasting increases your body's stress levels. This is nothing bad and just one of the body's reactions in maintaining your health. In fact, too little of is associated with inflammation, poor immune health, chronic pain, fatigue, and unstable blood pressure. The opposite is also the same as it is this abnormally high stress level that disrupt your body's reproductive cycle.

Now, the stress placed on the body by intermittent fasting does not reach the harmful levels. In fact, it contributes to the self-cleaning and self-repair effect caused by intermittent fasting through autophagy. But, each person's body is unique and would have a unique reaction to each situation. For intermittent fasting, it could be fasting beyond a certain timeframe would trigger unhealthy stress levels.

In addition to this, there are other factors that contribute to a person's stress levels such as lack of quality sleep, lack of or excess of exercise, and poor diet. Even if intermittent fasting alone does not cause you unhealthy amounts of stress, you can still reach such levels if other factors in your life are pushing making your life stressful.

Knowing these two causes already gives you a hint on how you can manage this unwanted effect by intermittent fasting. First, you must ensure that you are consuming enough protein in your diet. You can get what you need through red meat or through protein or amino acid supplements.

Second, you have to manage your stress levels. It could be as simple as getting enough sleep by going to bed early. In some cases, you might have to set up the conditions that can help you sleep better. You might also want to consider your lifestyle and eating habits. If any of these might contribute to elevated stress levels, you might have to change some of it to minimize stress. You can also alter your intermittent fasting schedule to shorter fasting phases. In this way, your body can adjust back from its stressful fasting phase sooner.

Hormones Go Beyond Your Fertility

Even if you do not plan on getting pregnant yet, your hormones should still concern you. The role of estrogen goes beyond your reproductive system. It also plays a role in your metabolism. And, if you want to create positive results with intermittent fasting, you better make sure that your metabolism is working as it should be.

Estrogen plays a role in modifying the amino acids that signal the release of hormones that make you feel full or hungry. It stimulates your neurons that starts or stops the regulation of your appetite. Moreover, if your estrogen levels drop, you are more likely feel hungrier than you actually are.

Intermittent Fasting for Pregnant Women

Many studies on fasting involve individuals following the Muslim tradition of Ramadan, which involves fasting from sun up to sun down. Some of the research participants are pregnant women who chose to fast even when they are exempted from doing so. What researchers found was that their insulin, glucose, and triglyceride levels improved. Furthermore, their babies have similar weights to the babies of mothers who did not fast (99).

However, it should be noted that there's a lower frequency in fetal movement for pregnant intermittent fasters. A low frequency of fetal movement is considered a warning sign regarding the baby's health. There is also not enough evidence suggesting that the infant did not experience adverse health effects that may appear later in life.

If you are considering intermittent fasting while pregnant, you must remember that it is during this time that your body needs to focus on helping your baby gain weight and develop its body, providing nutrients for brain development, and developing fat stores for breastfeeding.

It is important to first have a conversation with your doctor before attempting any kind of fast while pregnant. There are already doctor-approved methods that you can do to manage your weight. You can do moderate exercises such as walking, stationary cycling, and swimming. In fact, exercise can be good for you since it can shorten your labor, and reduce your risk for cesarean delivery and gestational diabetes.

For Women with Polycystic Ovarian Syndrome

Intermittent fasting can help those with polycystic ovarian syndrome (PCOS) lose weight. Those with PCOS find it difficult to lose weight due to their body's tendency to produce high insulin. Intermittent fasting helps improve this by improving their insulin sensitivity. This helps their body get better control on its insulin levels and indirectly assist in efforts to lose weight (100).

Furthermore, intermittent fasting can improve the chances of women with PCOS of getting pregnant. It can increase the levels of their luteinizing hormone, which one of the important hormones for your ovulation (101). And, with better chances for weight loss, PCOS women experience further benefits in their reproductive health by improving their menstrual cycle, fertility, and ovulation. The reduction in insulin resistance and cardiovascular disease risk also reduces the complications that women with PCOS are more likely to encounter during pregnancy and while giving birth.

Intermittent Fasting While Breastfeeding

Intermittent fasting can lower the milk supply of breastfeeding mothers (102). This is because of breastfeeding mothers not getting sufficient nutrients by doing an intermittent fast. To put this into perspective, those who are breastfeeding their child are advised to consume around 300 to 600 additional calories per day.

Furthermore, doing an intermittent fast will reduce the amount of food that you eat that contains the variety of macro and micronutrients. This can decrease the quality of the breastmilk. Although it may be not harmful, it can still cause potential risks in the future for the baby. According to a study, intermittent fasting can reduce the concentration of lactose and potassium, and the overall nutritional content of breastmilk.

Again, consult your doctor first if you are breastfeeding. You can still achieve weight loss or improve your insulin resistance through a healthy and well-balanced diet.

Intermittent Fasting During Post-menopause

Intermittent fasting can help women who are at their post-menopause stage. It can help post-menopausal women with their weight loss and management (103). The observed benefits include improved levels of total cholesterol, triglycerides, and fasting glucose.

Addressing Concerns About
Intermittent Fasting

It is not surprising that the concept of intentionally missing meals, which can last for a full 24 hours in some days, would raise some concerns. And, no one can blame those who are wary about intermittent fasting. After all, it goes against everything we believe and what is commonly known about nutrition and maintaining our health.

In order to put these worries to ease, here are some of the most common concerns about intermittent fasting. The answers that have been provided might have appeared in an earlier chapter. But, sometimes, these concerns are best answered directly and the best way to do it is by reiterating some points that have been previously made.

Is intermittent fasting safe?

Fasting has been around for years. Although intermittent fasting is being done for the purposes of one's health, religions have been practicing it as part of their spiritual traditions for centuries. These traditions have not caused serious health complications. Furthermore, both intermittent fasting and religious fasting have the same exceptions on who can and cannot do it.

Furthermore, your body has measures in place when you have no access to food in the form of body fat. It was how humans in before the advent of agriculture survived. They did not have the convenience of easily accessible food. In order to eat, they had to hunt or gather, which can sometimes take days before they can even do so.

Of course, this does not mean that you can immediately jump into intermittent fasting or start with 24-fasting phases. You would have to do it gradually until you can do the fasting phase that work best for your lifestyle or needs.

How can autophagy be good when it literally means "self-eating"?

The common belief seems to be is that nourishing our bodies is always good. This is true but only for the case of infants, toddlers, children, and teenagers. These are people who actually still have to grow. But, for the case of fully-grown adults, constant growth becomes harmful. Once a body reaches adulthood, balance (or homeostasis) should take priority.

Now, what does this have to do with eating and fasting? Well, as long as your body is metabolizing food, your body is in a state of growth. When everything you ate has been broken down and used up, your body will start a state of breaking down damaged and malfunctioning parts to fuel itself.

These two contrasting states maintain a balance within your body. If growth is unregulated, your body will get sick. Just look at cancer, it is simply uncontrolled growth of malfunctioning cells. This is the same for autophagy. If the body is left in a state of autophagy, the body would eventually deteriorate and experience various complications.

Will it slow down the body's metabolism?

You probably heard before that meal skipping or fasting can slow down your metabolism. This concept came from the belief that our bodies need three full meals per day. This is actually not the case.

To correct this belief, you must first know what "metabolism" actually means. It is just a term to describe all of the chemical reactions occurring in your body to maintain the life of your cells and your body. Now, from this definition alone, you will realize that autophagy is one of these reactions that can be counted as part of your metabolism.

In fact, although it might be taking the belief "meal skipping is bad" out of context, constantly feeding your body with calories and macronutrients is harmful for your body. It is always in a state of feeding that it does not have a change to achieve stability. And, as you have read in earlier chapters, constant supply of nutrients can cause adverse effects in your body. It can be in the form of insulin resistance, liver and kidney disease, and weight and fat gain.

Will it cause nutritional deficiency?

Nutritional deficiency does not have anything to do with the amount of food you consume. It has more to do with the quality of what you eat and what you absorb into your body. If you are limiting what you eat to only a few food items, you are most likely deficient in nutrients not found in what you eat. It would not even matter if you eat more than what you need since it would still not give your body all the nutrients it needs.

Although it is possible that you can experience nutritional deficiency in intermittent fasting, the cause behind it has more to do with what you eat than how often or when you eat. You can avoid it through proper monitoring of your diet and smart choices on what you eat. This is where eating a diet rich in vegetables and healthy fats with lean protein and moderate carbohydrates will help you. Such a diet will give you an adequate supply of macro and micronutrients that your body would need. If you are still in doubt, you can take nutritional supplements to fill in the nutritional gaps that you might be missing from your diet.

Can it cause eating disorders?

Intermittent fasting can provide a lot of benefits for your health. But, if it will cause something that can harm your health, it is best to avoid. People who are at risk, currently going through, or previously had eating disorders are advised to avoid intermittent fasting.

If you are unsure if you are at risk, you can check your family background if a family member had a history of an eating disorder. Other signs of eating disorder risk include perfectionism, impulsivity, and mood instability.

Will it make me feel weak?

The feeling of being low in energy or tired is common among those just starting intermittent fasting. This feeling is associated with your declining blood sugar as you are in the middle to the latter parts of your fasting phase. This is normal since your body has not yet adapted to using fat for its metabolism.

Also, the psychological effect of your beliefs is quite powerful. We have been fed with the belief that we need frequent meals for our well-being. It can make you feel worse than you actually are.

To overcome these, you just have to push through your first few days in intermittent fasting (provided that you do not have any health conditions like anemia and hypothyroidism). Your body will eventually adapt in a little more than a week. Once it does, you will feel the mental clarity and the increased energy associated with the body's fat-burning state. As for the psychological barrier, your mind will eventually learn to differentiate actual hunger from cravings.

It is important that you start with a time restricted fast like the 16/8 method. It is unreasonable to expect your body to not feel weak in a 24-hour fast if it is your first time in intermittent fasting. In some cases, it is even advised to start with an 8- or 10-hour fast. This will give you a better chance of sticking through your intended schedule for intermittent fasting.

Will it cause muscle loss?

Intermittent fasting can cause muscle loss. But, if you eat well and do intermittent fasting right, you can maintain your muscle mass while losing fat. It is advised that you consume adequate amounts of protein so your body has ample supply of amino acids to maintain its mass. Getting enough protein from your diet becomes even more important if you are working out while doing an intermittent fast. It will supply your body the amino acids that it needs to repair and grow its muscles during the eating phases of intermittent fasting.

In some cases that there was muscle loss, it was minimal and most of it only consists of what you would call water weight.

Is it safe to do this in the long-term?

Generally, intermittent fasting is safe to do in the long term for both men and women. It was how our bodies are wired. But, you have to make sure that you are getting all the nutrients that you need. Although it might be inconvenient, you can keep track of your macronutrient intake. And, since long-term intermittent fasting has less to do with weight loss and more to do with weight maintenance, you will just have to make sure that you are consuming enough to maintain your weight.

Furthermore, you have to listen to your body. If you feel and look well doing it, you can continue intermittent fasting. If you feel a lack of energy or appear to be losing weight, you have to check your diet and adjust accordingly. If you do not feel good about it at all, it would probably be best to decrease the time for your fasting phase or completely stop it.

Regarding the best method for long-term intermittent fasting, it is best to stick to the 16/8 method. This method is more realistic and doable in the long-term. It will give you the benefits that you can get from intermittent fasting while still getting the nourishment you require on a daily basis.

All of the answers provided in this chapter are no substitute to your doctor's expert opinion. We are not bioidentical and it would not be reasonable to expect the same exact experience would happen to you in intermittent fasting. What might work for you might not work for you and vise-versa. It is important that you set things straight first in regards to your health. If you are sure that you can go through this, then you can start slowly. If at any time you do not feel well and continue to do so even after trying for a week or so, it would probably be best to reassess your health and see if you have an existing health condition.

Individuals That Should Not Do Intermittent Fasting

Intermittent fasting requires a level of commitment that might be impractical for some situations. You can easily do it if you have done some kind of diet before and integrated it to your life successfully. Factors like work, family, and personal life can affect how you do intermittent fasting. If doing it will negatively affect how well you do in these areas of your life, you will find it difficult and could even cause repercussions in the said areas.

This does not mean that doing it is impossible. It will just be more difficult. You can work around these challenges and find out how to make it work. However, if working around these challenges is impossible or too difficult, intermittent fasting might not be for you. Your work, family, and personal life is not worth sacrificing, especially that there are alternatives to intermittent fasting.

Other than these lifestyle factors, you should also consider where you are in terms of your health. If you are pregnant, breastfeeding, or planning to conceive, do not even think of doing intermittent fasting. The same also applies for the following:

- Those with a history or currently have eating disorder/s

- Underweight individuals

- Type-1 diabetes patient

- Below 18 years of age

- Individuals taking prescribed medication

- People with insomnia

- People who are chronically stressed

- Employees in performance-oriented or physical-intensive jobs

- Employees that work the night shift

- People who have no experience with exercise or dieting

  Some of these are not actually health conditions. But, if these individuals did intermittent fasting, they would likely experience fatigue or underperform on their jobs.

If you find yourself included in this list that should not do intermittent fasting, you still have other options to lose weight. A calorie-restricted diet has similar weight and fat loss potential as intermittent fasting. If you are interested with the effects of autophagy for your health, you can also achieve the same effect through exercise, antioxidant supplementation, and the ketogenic diet.

Why Intermittent Fasting Is Better Than Other Diets

Now, if you passed the "test" from the previous chapter, you are probably ready to read on how to get started. But, if you are still on the fence about it, this chapter will tell you why intermittent fasting is the best option that you have for weight loss and general health.

Convenience

There are many different ways that you can do intermittent fasting. This makes it easy for you to make it fit your lifestyle or preferences. For example, if you are doing a 16/8 method, you can schedule your fasting phases from seven in the evening until 12 noon the next day. In this way, you can coast through your fasting phase asleep. You also do not have long to wait until you can eat for the next day. This set-up makes it easy for those just starting with a full intermittent fasting schedule.

Also, if you happen to miss the start of your fasting schedule, you can easily adjust the start and end of your fasting phase. Using the previous example, let us say that you went out with your friends and missed the start of your fast because of it. Although not ideal, you can shift your schedule and just count from the time you ended your last meal. In this way, you can still fully benefit from its benefits and you do not have to completely break your schedule.

The same can also be said for 5/2 and eat-stop-eat method. You can reschedule your fasting phase when an occasion comes up. You can't say not eat in these events. Doing so would be terribly rude to the hosts or your friends. It would also be difficult since everyone else around you would be eating.

You can also easily set your meal plans for intermittent fasting since there are no restrictions on what you can and cannot eat. All you have to remember are the times when you can start eating and when you have to stop. You can be strict and precise with what you eat but, even if you choose not to, you can still experience the benefits of intermittent fasting.

Benefits

Intermittent fasting is proven in helping people lose weight. It can even help maintain your muscle mass while shedding body fat. It also goes beyond weight loss, which is what most diets focus on. It prompts your body to undergo a natural process to clean and repair its cells, and to prompt reactions that help delay aging in your body. Because of this, even if you do not intend to lose, you can still benefit from intermittent fasting.

Can Accommodate for a Nutritious Diet

You can do intermittent fasting in your own terms. You can set up your diet to be at a caloric deficit to help in your weight loss. On the other hand, if you want to maintain your lean bodyweight or support your workout goals, you can set your diet at a caloric equilibrium or surplus. What's great about this is you can still experience autophagy in both cases. You would still benefit from intermittent fasting in some way.

Moreover, you do not have to restrict yourself from eating certain types of food. You can eat whatever you like: carbohydrates, protein, fat, or vegetables. Because of this, you can easily avoid experiencing nutritional deficiencies from your diet. Although it is discourage, you can even eat junk food since all the benefits from this results from intentional depletion of glucose and glycogen in your body.

The Different Methods of Intermittent Fasting and How Each Can Benefit You

You have already read in the first chapter the different methods that fall under intermittent fasting. In this chapter, you will be taking a closer look on each of those methods. You will learn how to do each method and from there you can see which one would work best for your lifestyle.

16/8 method

The 16/8 method is the most popular way to do intermittent fasting. It got its name from the 16 hours of fasting and 8 hours of eating involved. It is often called interchangeably as the Lean Gains method. But, for the sake of discussion, this book will consider the 16/8 method and the Lean Gains method as different methods of intermittent fasting. Although Lean Gains method is the original 16/8 method, the generic 16/8 method known today took on a life of its own that, if you ask someone what it is, it is completely different from what bodybuilder Martin Berkhan designed.

How to do the 16/8 method

Doing the 16/8 method is simple. You just have to pick an eight-hour window that would be the only time that you can eat for the day. You are free to decide when you want this eating period will start or end. Some might say that a certain time is the best to end a fast or to start one due to some claim regarding weight loss, muscle gain, or appetite suppression. But, there is no evidence stating or supporting their claims. Just set it according to what works best for your lifestyle and personal preferences.

During the eating phase, you are free to eat. The objective during this time is to give your body the nutrient and calories it needs. It is recommended to eat your well-balanced meals with equal intervals between each other. This will help stabilize your blood sugar as you would not gorge yourself of food and cause it to increase rapidly.

Once this time ends, you are prohibited from consuming or drinking anything that contains calories. This will last until the eating phase for the next day starts.

11. 14/10 variation for women

The 14/10 method is a variant of the 16/8 method. The two are almost exactly the same. The only difference is this method involves 10 hours for its eating phase and 14 hours for its fasting phase. It was created for women to prevent the negative effects of intermittent fasting done on their hormones. Also, the longer eating phase gives you more meals for the day. This can help in ensuring that you get enough nutrients, especially protein, to maintain a healthy hormone production in your body.

12. Lean Gains method

The Lean Gains method is the original form of the 16/8 method. Nutritional consultant, bodybuilder, writer, and personal trainer Martin Berkhan created it. It still operates with the same time restrictions of 16 hours of fasting and 8 hours of eating. However, unlike the 16/8 and 14/10 method, Berkhan instructs that the eating phase start at noon. This is to ensure that you are in a fed state during the afternoons and evenings. This schedule is meant to decrease the stress that you would get from work. Berkhan states that the eating phase can start later if you would be working late into the night.

Training is a big part of this method. It was formulated with the expectation that intermittent fasting would not stop a person's normal workout program. Because of this, this method can be done in four different ways. All were made with the consideration that each person would have different preferences on when and how they choose to schedule their workouts while doing intermittent fasting.

Furthermore, this method takes into account how diet and nutrient timing can help someone achieve their weight loss goals. However, unlike most diets, Lean Gains makes it easy since you only need to remember three things. First, you need to keep your caloric intake on the level that would help your reach your weight loss goal. Second, you need to eat fewer carbohydrates during non-workout days. Third, you need to follow the schedule and proportion of meals on your workout days.

For the workout days, the post-workout meal should consists of the majority of calories you would eat for the day. If the schedule allows for a pre-workout meal, it should provide the body with enough energy to do well in the workout. These should consist of 50 to 60 percent of carbohydrates and 40 to 50 percent of protein. The carbohydrate content would take care of your body's energy needs while the protein would maximize your muscle's protein synthesis and induce satiety. Fat is optional and can be used to add flavor to the pre-workout meal.

The key to the Lean Gains method is patience.

The Different Lean Gains Protocols

The protocols below only apply on workout days. If there is no workout, the protocols below do not apply and would follow a normal 16/8 method. There are a total of three meals for each eating phase and the last one is taken an hour before the eating phase ends.

The meal after the workout will always contain the most calories, carbohydrates, protein, and fat. The last meal always has the least amount of calories and carbohydrates with the exception of post-workout meals.

1. Fasted training

Training starts an hour before the eating phase starts. It is done on an empty stomach other than 10 grams of branch chain amino acids or of a similar mixture taken 5 to 15 minutes before the workout. The BCAA taken before the workout stimulates protein synthesis and metabolism. The small amount of amino acid is enough to halt the body's fasted state.

There is no pre-workout meal. The carbohydrate and calorie content of each meal decrease gradually as you go through the day.

2. Early morning fasted training

Training starts first thing in the morning after waking up. 10 grams of BCAA is taken 5 to 15 minutes before the workout. Another BCAA dose is taken an hour after training and another one at three hours after training.

3. One pre-workout meal

The first meal in the eating phase is the pre-workout meal. It consists around 20 to 25 percent of the day's total caloric intake. Workout is scheduled two to three hours after the pre-workout meal. Post-workout meal is schedule immediately after the workout.

This protocol is best for those who have the flexibility in their work or class schedule.

4. Two pre-workout meals

The first and second meal each has 20 to 25 percent of your total daily caloric intake. Training is done two to three hours after the second meal. Post-workout meal is taken an hour before the eating phase ends.

This is best for those who can only work out from five in the afternoon and until an hour before the eating phase ends.

You can adjust the Lean Gains method using the 14/10 fasting and eating schedule. You will still be fasting and benefit from the benefits of proper meal timing and nutrition of the Lean Gains method.

But, it could be best to try the Lean Gains method first by using the 16/8 eating and fasting schedule. You and your body would probably have easier time doing the fasting phases since you will be eating enough to satisfy your caloric needs so you would not be at a caloric deficit. Furthermore, the method places an emphasis on adequate protein intake. This ensures that you would get enough protein to supply what your body needs to produce hormones and to keep your reproductive cycle uninterrupted.

The Lean Gains method might look intimidating especially for an intermittent fasting method. The creator of this diet admits that it takes more work than your average fasting method. But, this is a much simpler approach compared to diets and strategies for those with goals of losing fat while building muscle. It also beats the other diets since Lean Gains method can be implemented using whatever type of diet you want. As long as you consume the right amount of calories, the right macronutrient proportions, and time your nutrient intake, it would not matter if you do a paleo, vegan, vegetarian, or Mediterranean diet.

Eat-Stop-Eat Method

Brad Pilon created this method while he was in his graduate studies. It was first introduced through his book "Eat Stop Eat."

The Eat Stop Eat method is done by fasting for 24 hours once or twice per week. The fasting phase can start any time as long it lasts for 24 hours before eating another meal. The 24 hours of fasting should be non-consecutive days if you choose to implement a two days per week fasting schedule.

This schedule would limit your calories to the amount you consume during the five or six days of the week that you can eat. This would put you automatically in a calorie deficit for the week. For example, if you consume around 2,000 calories per day, you would have a calorie deficit of 2,000 per week if you have one fasting phase per week, or 4,000 calories per week if you have two fasting phases per week.

During the eating phase, you will eat the amount of food that you would normally consume when you are not fasting. It is strongly advised to avoid making up for lost calories or bingeing on food after you end your fast. You should take the mindset that you will only consume what you normally eat in a day.

You are also free to choose what you eat. You can follow a diet to improve your health like the ketogenic diet, paleo diet, or a Mediterranean diet. But, you have to make sure that you are consuming enough to satisfy your caloric needs for the day. Also, these diets should not place additional stress on your self-control. Intermittent fasting is already hard as it is, especially for one that has a 24-hour fasting phase. Adding another factor like a diet will make it more difficult for you.

5:2 Method

The 5:2 method involves a fasting phase that restricts your food intake to 25 percent of your total caloric consumption. As its name suggests, this method involves five days of normal eating days and two days of fasting days. Although it recommends that women eat less than the calories indicated for fasting days, the chapter about differences between men and women indicate that their bodies should actually be eating more to avoid disruptions on their hormones. Because of this, it is best for women to consume around 28 to 30 percent of their total daily calories.

During fasting days, you can choose to eat what you would normally as long as you stay within the limits. But, if you want to avoid the feeling of hunger, you would have to be smart about what you eat. The best food choices during these two days are those that do not contain much calories but will make you feel fuller for quite a long time. These food items are green leafy vegetables, small cuts of roasted lean meats, soups, and salad.

You can set up three meals for your fasting days. But, based on other people's experience, a meal or two works best in managing their hunger or appetite. They also schedule these meals at lunch and dinner. They found it easier to skip breakfast than going without food lunch or sleeping without having eaten anything.

Unlike the Eat-Stop-Eat method, the creator Kate Harrison did not place any restriction on whether the fasting days can be done consecutively or not. However, she did state that fasting should not exceed 48 hours. She also does not recommend this method for pregnant women, nursing mothers, teenagers, children, and people with eating disorders. She also recommends anyone with diabetes or chronic medical conditions to first consult their doctor or specialist before doing the 5:2 method.

The method allows for exercising during fasting days. But, the calorie allowance for the day should be followed. Exercising would not allow to have additional calories so you can eat more food. If you do choose to exercise, you have to be careful and immediately stop once start feeling unwell.

You can vary the number of fasting days depending on what suits you best. Some people choose a 6:1 eating and fasting schedule if their lifestyle does not make it possible for 5:2 schedule or if they are just aiming to maintain their weight. You can also increase it to three fasting days as long as you do not exceed more than 48 consecutive hours of fasting.

You can choose to do this method for the long term. But, Harrison recommends to stick to a 5:2 or a 6:1 eating and fasting schedule.

Alternate Day Fasting (ADF)

The alternate day fasting is a method of intermittent fasting where in you would be completely restricted from food or calories every other day. If you would include the number of hours of your sleep to it, you will be fasting for 30 to 32 hours. From the number of hours involved fasting, this method is obviously not for beginners. It also involves going to bed after having a day without eating anything.

This is best for those looking to benefit from the effects brought by a fast-induced autophagy to the body. Most studies researching the effects of a fast-induced autophagy usually use the alternate day fasting to trigger autophagy in the body. If you are only interested in losing weight, this might not suit your goals due to its difficulty. Also, the other methods with shorter or fewer fasting phases already does fine in regards to weight loss.

If you still want to do this method, you have to keep in mind that this is an advanced method of intermittent fasting. People who have done alternate day fasting had to work their way to being able to do it for a length of time that will create results. Usually, the time frame is around four to six weeks. In order to last that long, they have to be already experienced with intermittent fasting. This experience is usually a year of doing 16/8, 5:2, or eat-stop-eat.

ADF is only done for the short term. It is not like the 16/8 or 5:2 method that you can do on the long-term. If you plan to continue on intermittent fasting, it is best to return to your previous method or pick another one that can be done long term.

Based on anecdotal evidence, experienced intermittent fasters who did alternate-day fasting did not feel weak or terribly hungry on fasting days. Although it was difficult at first, their hunger levels remained the same throughout the day. Hunger was no longer an issue around two to three weeks into alternate day fasting.

Those who regularly worked out were able to do so while doing ADF. Some took a strategic approach of eating the night before and working out first thing in the morning on their fasting day. However, most women felt terrible, especially if they had a workout, when they did not have enough protein or healthy fats during their previous eating day.

The Warrior Diet

The Warrior Diet is Ori Hofmekler's method for intermittent fasting. It attempts to mimic the way Paleolithic humans ate, which involves frequent eating of produce (fruits, nuts, and vegetables) during the day and feasting during the night with a hearty meal before going to sleep. Unfortunately, the original method is quite impractical with how complicated it went with the carbohydrate and calorie cycling involved, the restrictions placed on the diet to closely mimic a paleo diet, and the specified workout that should be done. For the case of this book, the Warrior Diet is stripped to its essentials to stay true to the regimented-approach of intermittent fasting. This modified version only involves 20 hours of fasting and 4 hours of eating every day.

You can schedule the eating phase whenever you want for the day. But, it is best to schedule it during the night – around 7 or 8 in the evening is the best time to start. This is for your body to wake up in a fasted state on the next day. Since your body is already in a fasted state, your insulin levels will be low and your body can enter a fat-burning state earlier in the day. As you go through your tasks for the day, you are burning fat. This will only stop during the eating phase when your body digests the carbohydrates from your only meal.

The Warrior Diet works best if you already follow a workout regimen. The workout is best done on a fasted state since it will maximize the amount of fat that your body metabolizes.

As for the time of the workout, it is more manageable to do it in the morning. Your meal the previous night will still fuel your body through your exercises.

Like Alternate Day Fasting, this method is not for beginners due to the 20-hour period of fasting from anything that contains calories. It is also a method designed for maximum weight loss. Therefore, this should only be done if you want to lose weight or fat. It is not done on the long term and should only last for four to six weeks. You would eventually have to switch to more sustainable method like the 5:2, 16/8, or Lean Gains method.

One Meal a Day (OMAD)

One Meal a Day, or OMAD, is a method of intermittent fasting that involves a fasting phase lasting for 23 hours and an eating phase lasting for only an hour. Its name is derived from how an hour is only enough a single meal. Similar to the Warrior Diet, it uses the premise that ancient civilizations, particularly the Romans, only ate a single large meal each day and that the modern diet is giving the body more than what it needs.

OMAD is done best with a meal that fully satisfies the body's needs. This satiety is an indication that the body got what it requires and can stop eating for the day. There are those who have done OMAD in the long-term and state that they feel fine and function well throughout the day. They can exercise normally. They feel more energetic and lighter compared to how they felt with a "normal" eating regimen or a shorter fasting regimen. They also rarely got sick and, if they do, their body responds and gets better faster.

On the other hand, there are those who state that it is not possible long-term and that they cannot exercise at all. But, most people who state these are those who did not stick to it for more than a week or so. They also seem to have jumped straight into One Meal a Day instead of starting with an easier intermittent fasting method.

Due to the nature of this method, those with health conditions are highly discouraged from using this method. It is best that they use methods with shorter fasting periods. Of course, they should first consult their doctor before doing so.

As for beginners, this will be a huge adjustment from eating at least three meals a day. It is best to start with a 16/8 method and work towards the OMAD method.

The Four Keys to Success with Any Intermittent Fasting Method

Regardless of your preferred method, you need four things to succeed in intermittent fasting – quality food, proper nutrition, consistency, and patience.

Good food quality

You are free to eat whatever you like in intermittent fasting. But, you experience better results if you nourish your body with quality calories from whole foods and not junk or processed items. Your body will get the nutrients it needs from good quality food. It is a better option than getting empty calories that would not do much in feeding your body beyond its metabolism.

Proper nutrition

Intermittent fasting is a weight loss strategy that does not focus much on adequate calorie consumption or balanced nutrition. This idea comes from the belief that the limited time window would force you to have fewer meals. There is also an assumption that you would not binge on food whenever you can and that you would listen to your body when full.

However, if you do binge on food during your eating phases, you will eat more than your body needs. It will place you at a calorie surplus and make your body slower in reaching a fasted state. This is also the same if you have more meals than you actually need during your eating window. Both of these would not benefit your efforts in your pursuit of weight loss. It could even be enough to increase your weight in methods with shorter fasting periods.

The opposite is also true. You cannot eat too little or else your body would not have enough nutrients for its needs. Your body needs more than calories or glucose for its metabolism. It needs protein to form amino acids, fat and oils for fatty acids, and vitamins and minerals to support your body's functions. If you do not get enough of these, your body will get sick. You can experience digestion problems, unusual food cravings, muscle weakness, palpitations, menstrual issues, sleepiness, and decreased mental function.

Consistency

You have to stick to a method for a period of time. You cannot expect results to happen after only a week of intermittent fasting. It takes at least one to three months of consistent effort in following a method to get the best results.

Patience

You have to be patient. Your body need time to adjust. You will experience difficulty at first due to how it adapts. Also, it will take some time to achieve your goals for weight loss, fat loss, or better body composition. Depending on your present situation, you might have to do shorter fasting phases before you can do one of the methods mentioned. You might also have to adopt intermittent fasting for a longer period to achieve weight loss.

The Food and Drink Guide for Intermittent Fasting

What not to eat or drink during intermittent fasting

While in a fasting phase, you are obviously restricted from eating anything that contains calories. When you enter the eating phase, you are free to eat whatever you want. But, if you want to lose your weight faster, you better avoid the following food and beverages listed below:

Anything Containing Refined and Added Sugar

Removing refined and added sugar in what you eat or drink is the first tip you would always get in any strategy to improve your health. Intermittent fasting is not different.

Sugar does not nourish your body in any way. It is only in what you eat and drink to add flavor. It can rapidly increase your blood sugar levels and elevate your insulin levels, which will make it difficult for you to lose fat.

Here are the food and drink that contain refined or added sugars:

- Energy drinks
- Soft drinks (even diet soda)

- Sweetened juices and fruit drinks

- Chewing gum

- Candy bars

- Sweets

- Pastries

- Sweetened chocolate

Alcoholic beverages

In terms of calorie content, you can drink a bottle of beer in your eating phase. But, if you consider what alcohol can do to your body, it is best to avoid it for the whole duration of your intermittent fasting. This is because of alcohol's ability to hinder fat burning in an individual.

Also, it can decrease your insulin sensitivity. Even drinking it during your eating phase can cause drawbacks to your progress, especially in improving your body's insulin sensitivity.

Processed food and canned goods

Processing and canning food are done to preserve food. To preserve food, large amounts of salt are added. Although salt does not contain significant calories, it stimulates your appetite and makes it difficult for you to sense if you already had enough food.

Furthermore, most processed food items are low in nutrients. Eating such items would only add calories but would not give your body precious vitamins, minerals, and antioxidants.

Simple carbohydrates

Simple carbohydrates are grains that have been stripped of its fiber and nutrients to make it taste or look better. In some cases, it is also done to improve its shelf life. It is a poor source of calories due to its low nutritional content. Also, simple carbohydrates are quickly digested and absorbed into glucose by the body.

Deep fried foods

Deep fried food items contain high levels of unhealthy fat and salt. It also contains high calories but low nutritional value, especially in the case French fries, potato chips, and similar food items.

Frozen meals

These meals contain high amounts of salt as a preservative. It is also pre-cooked and have likely lost a significant amount of its nutritional value because of it.

What to eat or drink during intermittent fasting

If it is not found on the previous list, you can eat or drink it. This list will not provide all items that you can eat or drink in intermittent fasting. Generally, as long as it is not on the "do not eat or drink" list, you can eat or drink it during your eating phases. The items mentioned below will be a few that you should eat more of while doing intermittent fasting (and while under a normal eating schedule). These food and drinks will help you have a healthier body and experience better results in intermittent fasting.

Whole carbohydrates

The best source of carbohydrates is those that have only been minimally processed. These still have their fiber intact and it did not go through a process that stripped it of its nutrients.

Moreover, because of its intact fiber, your body does not digest it as fast as simple carbohydrates. The body digests and absorbs it at a slower rate so your blood sugar levels would only experience a gradual increase.

Vegetables

Vegetables contain vitamins and minerals that support the various functions in your body. These also contain antioxidants that can induce autophagy for fighting toxins and suppressing free radicals in your body. Vegetables can help your digestion and make you feel fuller.

Water

It has no calories so you can drink it in both your fasting and eating periods. Aside from keeping you hydrated, it can reduce your hunger, maintain the health of your digestive system, regulate your body's temperature, and help flush out toxins and waste in your body.

But, avoid water that has been sweetened or artificially flavored. These contain sugars that would break you out of a fasted state.

Black coffee

By itself, coffee does not contain any calories. You can drink it during your fasting and eating periods. It can help manage your hunger by making you feel satiated.

But, drink coffee moderately when doing intermittent fasting since it enters your bloodstream on an empty stomach. Some coffee beans can make your stomach feel acidic if taken on an empty stomach. Avoid drinking more than two cups of coffee a day as it can cause anxiety, a jittery feeling, and weakness.

Tea

Like coffee, tea does not contain calories if drinking it without sugar or milk. It contains antioxidants that help manage free radicals and oxidative damage in your body. It also contains beneficial contents for your gut health and detoxification.

Milk

Milk is a great source of calcium, fat, and protein. It should be consumed in moderation. This is due to it containing lactose, which is a form of sugar. Avoid buying or drinking milk with added sugar in it.

Apple Cider Vinegar

Apple cider vinegar can prevent rapid glucose increase in your blood (104). It also contains acetic acid (105), which promotes fat burning and slows down the rate that your body stores fat.

Nuts

Almonds, cashews, hazelnuts, and walnuts contain a significant amount of good cholesterol and antioxidants. It's a great snack for your eating window.

Protein

Chicken, eggs, seafood, and beef are great sources of protein. Protein can give you better satiety and is a great way to feel fuller, especially for the first meal after your fast. It also provides your body with the amino acids for building and maintain muscles, and for regulating hormones.

Beans and legumes

Beans and legumes are great non-meat sources of protein. These are also rich in vitamins and minerals.

Medium chain triglyceride oil

Drinking medium chain triglyceride oil (or coconut oil) is a great way to break your fast. It does not contain carbohydrates but it suppresses your appetite. It provides your body energy through its fat content, which would be easily and immediately converted into ketone bodies. This influx of new fuel for the body would make your appetite more manageable as your break your fast. If you want to avoid overeating on your first meal, take one to two tablespoons of MCT oil or coconut oil at the start of your eating phase. After 30 minutes, you can start to eat your first meal for your eating phase.

Common Mistakes and How to Fix Them

A simple mistake can prevent you from benefiting from intermittent fasting. But, if you are making two or more of these mistakes, you are likely making things worse for your body by losing muscle mass or gaining weight. Here are the mistakes you want to avoid to prevent this from happening and how to fix them so you can actually lose weight.

Ignoring previous eating issues or disorders

There is nothing more harmful than the possible consequences if one chose to do an intermittent fast despite a history with eating disorders. Consult your doctor first before doing intermittent fasting. Also, seek alternative weight loss strategies that you can do.

Getting into it too fast

If this is your first weight loss plan, it is best to slowly get into intermittent fasting. Any diet or eating regimen will cause stress to your mind. If you are used to eating every two to four hours, you would not have a good experience jumping into a 16-hour fast immediately.

It is best to start with a shorter fasting period. You can start by reducing your number of meals. You can set a maximum number of meals for the day and set a schedule for it that you would follow. Once you get used to it, you can start by delaying your breakfast for a two to four hours in the morning. You can then adjust it until you reach the desired number of hours for your fasting period.

Not taking nutritional supplements

Regardless of how much food and variety is in your meals, it is difficult to acquire the full spectrum of vitamins and minerals for your body. You would need to take nutritional supplements if you want to your body to get the best nourishment. You can get what you would generally need from a daily multivitamin, a fish oil supplement (or similar omega-3 supplements), calcium supplement, and vitamin D supplement.

Eating too much carbohydrates and/or protein

Eating too many carbohydrates or protein than you need will cause your body to store excess energy into body fat. If you are not losing fat with intermittent fasting, you are probably making this mistake.

Generally, your total calorie intake for a day should consist of 45 to 65 percent of carbohydrates while 25 to 35 percent of protein. If you are aiming for fat loss, your carbohydrate intake should be lower while your protein consumption should increase.

Too much fat in the diet

If you eat too much fat, your body will prioritize burning the fat from your diet for energy. Again, you will find it difficult to lose weight and body fat if this is the case. To avoid this, keep your dietary fat intake to 20 to 35 percent of your total daily calories.

Eating too much calories

The intermittent fasting will put you on a calorie deficit. This is how you will lose fat. If you eat too much calories, you will find it difficult to lose fat and even experience weight gain.

To avoid eating too much, do not eat foods that will increase your appetite like keto bombs and salty food. You can also add more fiber and lean protein in your diet since it will help you feel more full.

Also, if you find yourself looking forward to breaking your fast, you might not be ready for your fasting schedule. Start with a shorter fasting period and gradually build it up.

Not enough calories

You do not need to restrict your calories in intermittent fasting. Your body will do it for you by feeling satiated after a meal. Restricting calories in intermittent fasting will just result in having too little calories available for your needs. Your body will respond by slowing down its metabolism, which will lead to weight gain.

The solution to this is to eat a meal with an amount close to how much you normally eat from a single meal without intermittent fasting.

Not enough water and salt or minerals

If you feel hungry but already had your meal, you are probably just thirsty. This is the stomach accumulating acid because it is empty for a long time. Drinking water prevents this accumulation and any complications caused by it.

However, you must balance this out with adequate salt intake by drinking a glass of water with a pinch of Himalayan pink salt at least once a day. It holds in the water you drink and prevent you from just eliminating it immediately through your urine.

Feeling too hungry

If you feel abnormally hungry in the middle or at the end of your fast, your fasting method is not suitable for your body's current state. This is usually the case for individuals who are not yet keto-adapted. This often results to overeating or eating anything even if its low quality calories.

To avoid this, start with a 10 or 12-hour fasting period and increase the time once you can go through it without being bothered by hunger.

Lack of exercise

Exercise provides a lot of benefits for your health. Not doing it due to intermittent fasting is the contrary to your pursuit of a healthier life. You have to figure out on how you can do it with intermittent fasting and just do it.

Walking and resistance training are the best form of exercise with intermittent fasting. Walking would not increase your stress levels while resistance training will increase your growth hormone production.

Stressful lifestyle

High emotional and physical stress will increase cortisol levels. If you combine this with intermittent fasting, you will like lose lean muscle mass, and gain weight from fat. This elevated stress is often a combination of poor sleep, poor stress management, and a busy lifestyle. If you cannot fix these causes for your increased stress, it might be best to handle these issues first before doing intermittent fasting.

Drinking Bulletproof coffee

Some would suggest that drinking Bulletproof coffee would not break your fast. But, this belief is completely wrong. Bulletproof coffee contains butter and MCT oil. Both of these contain calories,

Drinking Bulletproof coffee will not break your fast since it does not change your blood sugar levels. But, it will stop you from losing weight. Since you introduced butter and MCT oil into your body as sources of fat, the body will stop using your body fat to make ketone bodies for energy.

Repetitive eating pattern

Your body will eventually get used to your intermittent fasting method. Once it gets used to it, you will eventually stop progressing in losing weight. This is easily solved by switching to the other intermittent fasting methods in this book. It is important that you keep your body guessing and prevent it from getting used to a routine.

Getting Started with Intermittent Fasting

You now know what you need to get started. This chapter will take you through the steps so you can do intermittent fasting successfully in the short-term and on the long-term.

1. Identifying your goals

Before you start intermittent fasting, you must identify what you want to achieve from it. Whether you want to lose weight or have a better body composition, you would have to be specific about it. How much weight do you want to lose? How much lean muscle mass do you want to gain? How much body fat percentage do you want to end up with?

By identifying the specifics, you can gauge how much work you need to do to get there. It can give you a realistic timeframe on when you can achieve it if you stay consistent and do the right things.

You can also see if you would have to do the methods with the longer fasting periods eventually. You can even set a plan ahead of time so you can work towards the more advanced methods from day one of your intermittent fasting journey.

2. Know your daily calories

Intermittent fasting will only work if you know how much calories your body needs on a daily basis. You can find caloric intake calculators on the internet. These would give you an estimate based on your age, height, weight, gender, and activity level. Some calculators will also provide a daily amount for each macronutrient.

You will then divide this amount by how many meals you have per day. This would give you how much calories each of your meals should contain. You will use this to estimate how much you should eat for each meal while intermittent fasting.

This value is just an estimate. Actual calorie requirements vary on how your day is going. You would have to observe and feel how your body is doing. For example, if you are feeling too weak, you might be not eating enough. Or, if you are gaining weight, you are probably eating too much. From these observations, you can learn how to adjust your meals.

3. Pick a method that works best for you

The most suitable intermittent fasting method for you is not the one that would give you the fastest results. But, it is the method that you can consistently do long enough to reach your goal. If you are just starting out, it is best to begin with the 16/8 method or its variants – 14/10 method or the Lean Gains method. If you already have experience in intermittent fasting or have become comfortable with the 16/8 method, you can start aiming for doing the methods with the longer fasting periods like the One Meal a Day, Warrior Diet, 5:2 method, and eat stop eat. Once you have become comfortable with 20 to 24-hour fasts, you can then move on to alternate day fasting.

To avoid placing too much stress on your body, it is best to revert back to the 16/8, 14/10, or Lean Gains method if you plan to change your method to another fasting method. Most intermittent fasting enthusiasts use the 3 methods with 16 hours or less of fasting phase as their long-term methods. They use is as a way to bridge between methods that involve longer fasting hours or long and frequent fasting phases.

4. Set yourself up for success

Before you get started, you first have to prepare yourself and your environment for succeeding in intermittent fasting. The first step you must take is removing all the food and drinks included in the "do not eat or drink" list in this book. Switch these out for items included in the "eat or drink" list. You might have to talk to your family, roommate, or partner about this if you are living with them. Doing so will help you avoid temptation while in an intermittent fast.

Next, start getting enough sleep. It will make your intermittent fast more easy and effective. You also have to stop snacking and focus on getting your caloric needs from your meals. It will also help to gradually remove refined and added sugar from your diet. Applying these two fixes to your diet would make the first two weeks of your intermittent fast easier.

As you are doing these fixes, you can start scheduling your meals. This will help you get used to only eating at a certain time. For example, you can set all meals to have at least four hours interval. You can also restrict meals at a certain length of time like you can't eat between 8pm until 8am the next day. In this way, you are training yourself to be above the influence of your appetite or hunger.

5. Get started

Now that you have prepared yourself, you can now get started with intermittent fasting. You can immediately go straight to a 16/8 method if you find it easy skipping breakfast. But, it is also fine to transition into it, or a 14/10 method, by slowly increasing the time between your dinner the previous night and your first meal for the day.

However you choose to get started, it will be difficult at first. This is new for your body. You might not feel it on your first day but you will feel hunger during your first week. Just be patient and consistently follow the method that you set for yourself.

During your fasting phase, keep yourself hydrated. When you enter your eating phase, break your fast with nutrient-rich vegetables, lean meat, and fiber-rich whole carbohydrates. Continue this with the rest of your meals and snacks by getting most of your calories from items listed in the previous chapter. You must also take nutritional supplements to ensure that you are getting enough of the essential nutrients that your body needs.

6. Observe, feel, and adapt

Even if you research on medical journals and other people's experiences, you will still have to learn firsthand on how your body reacts to intermittent fasting. This is why you have to start slow so you can see if your body is taking it well. A gradual approach will also make it easier for you to change your plans, adjust your diet, or shift your fasting periods.

You must also keep track of your progress. Take note of your weight, muscle mass, and fat loss. If you are doing resistance training, you can compare how you did before and after you started intermittent fasting. You can also keep track the difference on how you progressed in your training. And, if you find that you are plateauing in your progress, you can choose if you want to take it further, change your goal, or maintain your current state. From there, you can start all over again in choosing a new method for more progress or a method for long-term intermittent fasting.

Doing Intermittent Fasting with a Ketogenic Diet

The ketogenic diet helps your body maintain a fat-burning state. It consists of low carbohydrate, moderate protein, and high fat proportions. This dietary composition causes similar benefits to intermittent fasting since it uses the same mechanics of reducing insulin resistance, stimulating fat metabolism, and promoting autophagy in the body. Because of their similar effects, you might find yourself wondering if you can do both at the same time.

The short answer to this is YES. You can combine the keto diet and intermittent fasting. But, it will be difficult. So, it is best that you have consistently done one of these two for a few months before combining it with the other. Here are the rules that you have to follow for a ketogenic diet:

- Macronutrient proportions are at 75 percent fat, 20% protein, and 5% carbohydrates.

- Macronutrient proportions are based on a person's daily caloric needs to maintain weight.

- You are restricted from food and beverage containing sugar, simple carbohydrates, alcohol, citrus, and fructose.

- Other forms of sugar are not allowed, such as maple syrup, honey, coconut sugar, and agave syrup.

- Starchy vegetables, beans, legumes, grains, and grain products are not prohibited.

- Unhealthy fats, like margarine and vegetable oils, should be avoided.

- Processed and packaged foods are not allowed.

- Food and drinks with sweeteners, preservatives, and artificial coloring in the ingredients should be avoided.

When combining a ketogenic diet with intermittent fasting, you have to make sure that you are getting enough calories and nutrients. You have to be sure that you are eating enough calories. Since you will be restricted from eating carbohydrates, you have to place an emphasis on your diet for nutrient-dense keto-approved food items. These include food high in healthy fat like avocado, high quality animal and plant source of protein, coconut oil, and leafy green vegetables.

Furthermore, you have to closely track the levels of your ketone bodies. You need to stay in ketosis without reaching the levels that indicate diabetic ketoacidosis (240 mg/dl). Because of this risk, you need to use glucose meters with a ketone measurement feature. Warning signs of diabetic ketoacidosis include vomiting for more than two hours, queasy feeling, stomachache, fruity breath, difficulty breathing, tiredness, dizziness, and confusion.

Lastly, you have to take a similar approach to how you started intermittent fasting. You have to take it slow. In this case, you will gradually decrease carbohydrates in your diet. This will help your body get used to having no access to carbohydrates and to being in an almost constant state of ketosis.

The same precautions from intermittent fasting apply in this combination with the keto diet. You have to observe how your body is doing. You have to make sure that you do not feel like you are not getting enough calories. You also have to ensure that you feel well doing it. Lastly, you have to adjust the diet and the fasting length if you ever find it necessary to do so.

Intermittent Fasting Shopping List

Meat

Meat will provide your body with the protein it needs. The best meats that you can incorporate in your diet are lean red meats like beef, pork, mutton, and venison. These particular meats are rich in Vitamin B12. It is best to choose unprocessed meats since processed ones are high in salt and lower in micronutrient content.

Although it's not meat, eggs should be part of your list. This is an excellent source of protein and is quite versatile for different recipes.

Vegan Sources of Protein

If meat is not something you wish to eat, there are plant-based sources of protein. Soy-based products are one of the highest sources of plant-based protein. There's also lentils, chickpeas, and beans that are not only versatile food items but also contain fiber, potassium, and iron.

As for vegetables, you can find significant amounts of protein in kale, mushrooms, and broccoli. There are also seeds high in protein such as hemp seeds and chia seeds, and grain like quinoa and seitan.

- Tofu

- Edamame

- Tempeh

- Beans

- Green or red lentils

- Chickpeas

- Chia seeds

- Hemp seeds

- Quinoa

- Seitan

Vegetables

Vegetables contain vitamins and minerals that support your metabolism. This metabolism should be at its best shape if you want to lose weight. Buy vegetables that contain the most number and variety of micronutrients for your body.

- Asparagus

- Beet root

- Broccoli

- Carrot

- Cauliflower

- Celery

- Chili peppers

- Lettuce

- Pumpkin

- Spinach

Fish and seafood

Fish are rich in omega-3 fatty acids. It is essential for you're the health and function of your bones, brain, and heart. The best sources for this fat include sardines, mackerel, tuna, anchovies, and wild salmon.

Vegan sources of omega 3 fatty acids

Omega 3 fatty acids are a part of a healthy diet. Fortunately, there are vegan sources available that can provide a comparable amount to fish.

- Chia seeds

- Edamame

- Seaweed

- Kidney beans

- Hemp seeds

- Flaxseeds

- Walnuts

Nutritional Supplements

Your body does not stop needing the micronutrients it requires. Unfortunately, it is very difficult to get all of vitamins and minerals you need through only your diet. You have to take nutritional supplements if you want your metabolism and your body at its best.

- Daily multivitamin for vitamins and minerals

- Omega-3 supplement of your choice

- Vitamin D

- Calcium

If you are doing the Lean Gains method, you would also need a BCAA supplement and Whey protein for your pre-workout.

Dairy

Dairy is an excellent source of protein, calcium and fat. The best dairy products are those that went through very minimal processing.

- Organic dairy

- Cottage cheese

- Yogurt

- Greek yogurt

Fats

Fats are a great way to satisfy your appetite and make you feel fuller. Furthermore, using these oil in your diet will give your body nutrients. Some of these are also better cooking oils for cooking the recipes in the next chapter.

- Coconut Oil (and/or MCT oil)

- Heavy cream

- Olive oil

- Butter

Fruits

Fruits contain vitamins and fibers. It's. a great snack in between meals. Since it does not contain much calories, you do not have to worry about overeating because of snacks in your eating phases.

- Apple

- Avocado

- Banana

- Berries

- Grapefruit

- Grapes

- Lemon (to flavor water or for salads)

- Melon

- Orange

Beverages

Non-caloric beverages are a great way to ease your mind during your fasting phase.

- Green tea

- Black tea

- Herbal tea

- Coffee (unsweetened and no cream or dairy)

Intermittent Fasting Recipes and Meal Plans

Essential Intermittent Fasting Recipes

Smoothies

13. Avocado Breakfast Smoothie

Serving size: 1

Total calories: 1,099

Carbohydrates: 42.6g

Fiber: 27.8g

Fats: 104.6g

Protein: 14.1g

Ingredients

- 1 avocado

- 1 cup coconut milk

- 1 cup spinach or kale

- 1 handful blueberries

- 1 tablespoon chia seeds

Instructions:

Blend all the ingredients.

14. Avocado Protein Shake

Serving size: 1

Total calories: 564

Carbohydrates: 21.3g

Fiber: 8.6g

Fats: 42.6g

Protein: 31.2g

Ingredients

- ½ avocado

- 1 handful spinach

- ½ cup water

- ½ cup milk

- 1 scoop protein powder

- 1 tablespoon fresh parsley

- 1 tablespoon coconut oil

- 1 tablespoon walnuts

- 1 teaspoon cacao powder

- 1 teaspoon cinnamon powder

- 1/3 teaspoon sea salt

Instructions

Put all the ingredients in a blender. Blend for 1 minute.

15. Cashew Milkshake

Serving size: 1

Total calories: 398

Carbohydrates: 53.3g

Fiber: 6.8g

Fats: 17.6g

Protein: 14.3g

Ingredients

- 1 medium banana

- 1 cup soy milk

- 3 tablespoons cashews

- 3 teaspoons cacao powder

- A pinch of Himalayan salt

  Instructions

Put all the ingredient in a blender. Blend.

Meals

16. Banana and toasted oatmeal

Serving size: 1

Total calories: 700

Carbohydrates: 100.4g

Fiber: 11.3g

Fats: 24.7g

Protein: 24.2g

Ingredients

- 1 cup rolled oats
- 1 ½ cup milk
- ½ tablespoon butter
- 1 banana, sliced

Instructions

1. Heat a pot over medium heat.
2. Add and melt the butter. Toast the rolled oats.
3. Once toasted, add the milk and boil.

4. Reduce the heat to low once it boils. Simmer for three minutes while stirring occasionally.

5. Transfer to a bowl and add the sliced banana. Serve.

17. Beans and Brown Rice

Serving size: 4

Total calories: 271

Carbohydrates: 47.8g

Fiber: 8.8g

Fats: 5.3g

Protein: 10g

Ingredients

- 15 oz black beans, undrained

- 14.5 oz stewed tomatoes

- 1 ½ cups instant brown rice

- 1 onion, chopped

- 1 tablespoon olive oil

- ½ teaspoon garlic powder

- 1 teaspoon dried oregano

Instructions

1. Heat olive oil on a small pot over medium high heat.

2. Add onion and cook until translucent. Add the beans and tomatoes. Stir.

3. Add the oregano and garlic powder. Stir then bring to a boil.

4. Once it boils, add and stir in the brown rice. Cover and reduce heat. Simmer for five minutes.

5. Remove from the heat and let it rest for five minutes.

6. Serve with your choice of protein.

18.Liver Burgers

Serving size: 1

Total calories: 947

Carbohydrates: 13.2g

Fiber: 0.3g

Fats: 39g

Protein: 129.4g

Ingredients

- ½ pound ground beef

- ½ pound ground beef liver

- ½ teaspoon cumin powder

- ½ teaspoon garlic powder

- Salt and pepper to taste

- Olive oil

Instructions

1. Mix all of the ingredient in a bowl

2. Heat olive oil on a skillet over medium-high heat

3. Cook the burgers to desired doneness.

4. Serve with salad or with whole wheat burger buns and preferred salad dressing.

19.Scrambled Eggs with Smoked Salmon

Serving size: 2

Total calories: 471

Carbohydrates: 22.2g

Fiber: 6.1g

Fats: 31.6g

Protein: 27.5g

Ingredients

- 8 midi vine tomatoes, halved

- 3 large eggs

- 1¼oz smoked salmon, roughly chopped

- 1 tbsp chopped chives

- 1oz fresh watercress, to serve

- 1 tablespoon olive oil

- freshly ground black pepper to taste

Instructions

1. Season the halved tomatoes with pepper. Heat the olive oil on a pan over medium heat. Cook the tomatoes until soft while stirring but without breaking.

2. Scramble the eggs and season with pepper. Add the salmon and chives.

3. Pour the scrambled egg mixture into the pan and cook it gently while stirring gently. This would take around three to four minutes. Remove from the heat and continue the gentle stir.

4. Add the watercress and serve.

20. Salmon and Roasted Vegetables

Serving size: 1

Total calories: 983

Carbohydrates: 7.9g

Fiber: 0.4g

Fats: 67.4g

Protein: 90.4g

Ingredients

- 1 pound salmon or other fish of choice
- 2 tablespoons fresh lemon juice
- 2 tablespoons ghee
- 4 cloves garlic, finely diced
- ½ cup vegetable of choice
- 1 tablespoon coconut oil

Instructions

1. Preheat the oven at 400 F.
2. Mix the diced garlic, ghee, and lemon juice.
3. Place the salmon in foil and pour the mixture on top.
4. Wrap and seal the salmon in the foil.
5. Place it on a baking sheet with the vegetables.

6. Drizzle the vegetables with coconut oil.

7. Roast for 15 minutes or until the salmon is cooked through.

21. Easy and Healthy Chicken Recipe

Serving size: 4

Total calories: 255

Carbohydrates: 16.4g

Fiber: 0.7g

Fats: 8.3g

Protein: 28.3g

Ingredients

- 4 skinless and boneless chicken breast, halved
- 1 onion, chopped
- 3 tablespoons tomato paste
- 2 tablespoons soy sauce
- 2 tablespoons lemon juice
- 1 teaspoon ground black pepper
- 2 tablespoons olive oil

Instructions

1. Heat olive oil over medium high heat.

2. Sauté onion. Once it becomes translucent, add chicken and brown on all sides.

3. Combine and mix the tomato paste, soy sauce, lemon juice, and pepper.

4. Pour over the chicken and bring to a boil. Cover and simmer for 25 to 30 minutes.

5. Serve with beans and brown rice or salad/

22. Easy Beef Stir-fry

Serving size: 4

Total calories: 255

Carbohydrates: 16.4g

Fiber: 0.7g

Fats: 8.3g

Protein: 28.3g

Ingredients

- 1 pound beef sirloin, cut into 2 to 2.5 inch strips

- 1 ½ cups of fresh broccoli florets

- 1 red bell pepper, cut into thin sticks

- 2 medium carrots, thinly sliced

- 1 green onion, chopped

- 2 tablespoons soy sauce

- 2 tablespoons toasted sesame seeds

- 1 teaspoon minced garlic

- 1 tablespoon olive oil

Instructions

1. Heat olive oil on a large skillet over medium-high heat.

2. Cook the beef until brown. Move the beef to the side and add the broccoli florets, carrots, bell pepper, garlic, and green onion on the center.

3. Cook while stirring vegetables for two minutes

4. Mix the beef and the vegetables. Add soy sauce and sesame seeds. Mix well until vegetables become tender.

5. Serve with salad or beans and brown rice.

23. Tuna Salad Bowl

Serving size: 1

Total calories: 866

Carbohydrates: 16.7

Fiber: 10.3g

Fats: 71.3g

Protein: 44.2g

Ingredients

- 120g canned tuna, drained
- ½ avocado, sliced
- 1 large handful watercress, washed and dried
- 1 large egg, boiled, peeled, and halved
- ¼ red onion, finely sliced
- 10 walnuts, halved
- 10 putted black olives
- 1 tablespoon mayonnaise
- 1 tablespoon olive oil
- 1 teaspoon sesame seeds
- Pepper to taste

Instructions

1. Preheat the oven to 400 F.

2. Place the walnuts on a baking sheet and roast for 6 to 8 minutes or until golden. Take it out of the oven to cool.

3. Place the watercress in a bowl. Add the olives, egg, avocado, and walnuts.

4. Mix the olive oil and mayonnaise. Drizzle the mixture on the contents of the bowl.

5. Add the tuna and sprinkle the sesame seed on the salad. Season with pepper to taste.

Recipes for a Ketogenic Diet

Delicious Cauliflower Rice

Serving size: 1

Total calories: 1011

Carbohydrates: 104g

Fiber: 24.4g

Fats: 54g

Protein: 42.4g

Ingredients

- 24 oz cauliflower florets
- 6 oz broccoli florets, chopped

- 2 carrots, peeled and grated
- 2 large eggs, beaten
- ½ cup corn
- ½ cup peas
- 2 green onions, thinly sliced
- 2 cloves garlic, minced
- 1 medium onion, diced
- 2 tablespoons low sodium soy sauce
- 1 tablespoon sesame oil
- 1 tablespoon freshly grated ginger
- 2 tablespoons olive oil, divided
- ½ teaspoon sesame seeds
- ¼ teaspoon white pepper

Instructions

1. In a food processor, pulse the cauliflower until it is broken down to a similar appearance as rice. Set aside.

2. Whisk the soy sauce, sesame oil, ginger, and white pepper in a small bowl. Set aside.

3. Heat half of the olive oil in a medium skillet over low heat. Cook the scrambled eggs until

completely cooked through. Flip once to cook the other side. Transfer to a plate and let it cool. Dice the cooked scrambled egg once cool. Set aside.

4. Heat the rest of the olive oil in the skillet at medium high heat. Saute the garlic and onion. Once the onions become translucent, add the the broccoli, corn, carrots, and peas. Stir constantly the contents until the vegetables become tender.

5. Add the cauliflower rice, and the mixture of green onions, eggs, and soy sauce. Continuously stir until the cauliflower rice becomes tender. This means that all of the contents have been heated through.

6. Garnish with sesame seeds. Serve while hot.

Greek Garlic Chicken

Serving size: 4

Total calories: 338

Carbohydrates: 6.2g

Fiber: 2.4g

Fats: 19.2g

Protein: 35g

Ingredients

- 1 pound chicken thighs

- ½ pound asparagus, ends removed

- 3 cloves of garlic, minced

- 3 tablespoon olive oil, divided

- 1 zucchini, sliced in half moon shapes

- 1 teaspoon oregano

- 1 lemon, juiced

- 1 lemon sliced

- Salt and pepper to taste

Instructions

1. Combine 2 tables spoons of lemon juice, olive oil, oregano, and minced garlic in a large-sized bowl. Whisk until combined.

2. Toss the chicken thighs into the bowl and coat it with the mixture. Cover the bowl with plastic wrap and marinate the chicken in the refrigerator. Take it out after 2 hours.

3. Season both sides of the chicken thighs with salt and pepper.

4. Preheat the oven to 425 F. Heat the rest of the olive oil in an ovenproof skillet over medium high heat. Place the chicken thighs on the skillet with

the skin-side down. Pour the marinade onto the skillet.

5. Let the skin-side of the chicken thighs become golden (10 minutes). Flip the chicken thighs then add the asparagus, lemon slices, and the zucchini.

6. Transfer the skillet to the oven. Cook for 15 minutes, or until the chicken gets thoroughly cooked and the vegetables become tender.

Keto Omelet

Serving size: 4

Total calories: 288

Carbohydrates: 6.8g

Fiber: 1.3g

Fats: 23.9g

Protein: 12.9g

Ingredients

- 2 medium eggs

- ¼ cup diced tomatoes

- ¼ cup diced onion

- ¼ cup shredded lettuce

- 2 tablespoons cream, full fat
- 1 tablespoon butter

Instructions

1. Whisk the eggs, cream, tomatoes, onion, and lettuce in a bowl.

2. Heat the frying pan over low medium heat.

3. Melt the butter in it and pour the egg mixture. Swirl the frying pan to evenly spread the egg in the skillet.

4. Cover the skillet with a lid and let it cook for two minutes.

5. Remove the lid, and use a spatula to transfer from the pan on to the plate.

Keto Beef Stroganoff

Serving size: 10

Total calories: 353

Carbohydrates: 3.4g

Fiber: 1g

Fats: 23.5g

Protein: 30.1g

Ingredients

- 3 pounds fat-trimmed beef brisket, cut against the grain into half-inch pieces

- 1 white onion, finely chopped

- 16 oz fresh mushrooms sliced

- 1 /12 cups beef broth

- ¾ cup sour cream

- ¼ cup mayonnaise

- ¼ cup avocado oil

- 2 teaspoons minced garlic

- 2 teaspoons ground thyme

- 2 tablespoon apple cider vinegar

- 1 ½ teaspoon xanthan gum

- ¾ teaspoon salt

- ½ teaspoon black pepper

Instructions

1. Heat a large saucepan over medium heat. Add the avocado oil, finely chopped onions, and minced garlic into it. Sauté contents for 3 minutes or until fragrant.

2. Add the cut beef brisket pieces, pepper, salt, and thyme. Sauté contents for 8 minutes or until beef is cooked. Make sure to stir frequently so the beef is browned evenly.

3. Turn down the heat to medium low. Add the beef broth and apple cider vinegar into the large saucepan. Simmer the contents for 30 minutes. Do not cover.

4. Add the mushrooms. Cover the pan and simmer for an hour and 30 minutes.

5. Remove the saucepan from the heat. Stir in the sour cream and mayonnaise in increments of a ¼ teaspoon. Incorporate it completely into the contents of the saucepan.

6. Add the xanthan gum until the liquid contents thicken.

7. Cover the saucepan with a lid and let it sit for 10 minutes.

8. Once the ten minutes is done, serve in bowls.

Meal Plan

You can use the smoothies in the provided recipes to break your fast. These are low carbohydrate meals that can be quickly digested and absorbed. Moreover, since these are high in fat, you will feel fuller compared to a regular meal.

If you prefer an actual meal to break your fast, you can do the oatmeal recipe. It consists of whole carbohydrates so it will not be absorbed easily by your body.

As for the rest of your eating phase, you can eat the other meals. These contain enough calories to bring up your total to 2,000 calories. You can adjust it according to your personal daily calorie intake.

Even if you are using a method that only allows for a single meal or a short eating phase, you can use these recipes and still get your required calories. You can choose a meal with meat or fish and combine it with a salad or the beans and rice. If you are still hungry, you can make a smaller portion of one of the smoothies.

If you are following the lean gains method, you can use one of the smoothie recipes as a pre-workout meal. However, you have to reduce the amount to coincide with the methods' limits. You can aside the rest for your post-workout meal.

Conclusion

Intermittent fasting provides women a simpler and more convenient method of losing weight. If done right, it also serves as a better weight management plan in the long term. It does not diminish the body's metabolism rate unlike in calorie restrictive diets that result in the body adapting a slower rate of metabolism. Because of this, women using this are less likely to experience the yoyo effect from most weight-loss diets.

What is great about intermittent fasting is that it goes beyond helping people lose weight. It triggers the body's natural self-cleanup and repair process known as autophagy. It places the body into a balance with the state of growth it constantly experience with the modern diet and lifestyle. Because of this balance, the body is at a lower risk for diseases associated with today's diet and lifestyle.

People who did intermittent fasting have experienced great benefits for their health. Several studies have observed improvements on people with high blood pressure, type 2 diabetes, high insulin resistance, metabolic syndrome, neurodegenerative disorders, and cardiovascular disease. Aside from managing these conditions, researchers have also observed intermittent fasting of helping those at risk for these degenerative diseases reduce their chances of preventing them. Even those who are not at risk experience benefits from their health, normal healthy individuals help their body fight aging, improve its immunity from infectious diseases, and increase its energy levels through intermittent fasting.

Despite these benefits for women, this book does not gloss over fact that it has risks. It recognizes the conditions unique to women that intermittent fasting could aggravate. The most important one discussed in this book is how the eating regimen affects hormone production. Although it eventually continues to its normal rhythm, small interruptions are enough to cause issues for the fertility, menstruation cycle, and overall reproductive health of women. It might seem small for those who are not planning to get pregnant soon. But, these hormones also affect other aspects of the body's health.

Fortunately, this risk is easily managed. It just requires an adequate protein intake that maintains one's hormonal balance. If this is not enough, adjustments to the time and frequency of fasting phases can also be done. Overall, contrary to what critics say, it is not a deal breaker for intermittent fasting but just something to be aware of.

Compared to other weight loss strategies, intermittent fasting is the least restrictive. In fact, one can say that no other diet or eating regimen compares to the amount of flexibility it allows. Beginners do not have to do something that they find to be too difficult. They can do a method that suits their current state of health, keto-adaptation, or lifestyle, and they would still benefit from intermittent fasting. Likewise, more advanced intermittent fasters have options to prevent a plateau in their efforts for weight loss. They can adjust their current method to lengthen or increase their fasting periods. Or, they can choose another method that would force their body to adapt to a new pattern.

Moreover, intermittent fasting can be tweaked to accommodate a person's lifestyle. If they cannot fast due to their work, they can adjust the fasting phases to accommodate their responsibilities. If they have health goals that require more caloric intake, they can increase their calories but they would still benefit from the effects of fasting. Even those who cannot do the full intermittent fasting experience can use its concept by scheduling their meals at only certain times. Basically, it is just your schedule for eating. It just turns out that it provides these amazing benefits for your body.

Of course, this book did not leave you merely knowing things about intermittent fasting. It provided you some of the priceless information that other intermittent fasters have experienced. The book revealed the common mistakes of those who failed in this regimen and provided the possible solutions of those who succeeded to overcome or prevent the said mistakes. It also provided what women should watch out for due to their dietary needs and solutions that they can apply for a successful and healthy intermittent fast.

You also know the steps to take so that you can get started with intermittent fasting. You know the importance of setting your goal. You were provided some strategies on how to help your body adjust to fasting phases even before you get started.

The steps on how you can start intermittent fasting

Important health considerations were also brought up and the risk when intermittent fasting is concerned. Moreover, common mistakes when doing intermittent fasting is discussed and some suggestions for solutions were given.

With the knowledge provided and the actionable information provided in this book, you can now take on the task of getting yourself ready and getting started with intermittent fasting. You know what to and what not to eat and drink so you will keep your eating and phases on point for your goal and your overall health. You also have the knowledge of what to watch out for, and how to adjust your regimen to avoid mishaps and succeed in achieving your goal. The only that is missing is you getting started.

Everything that you have learned from this book is worthless if you do not use it. You can start by attempting your first 12 hour fast and see how it feel. Or, you can start timing your meals so you only eat during the time you specify for yourself. However you choose to get started, the important thing is that you start.

Thank you

Before you go, I just wanted to say thank you for purchasing my book.

You could have picked from dozens of other books on the same topic but you took a chance and chose this one.

So, a HUGE thanks to you for getting this book and for reading all the way to the end.

Now I wanted to ask you for a small favor. ***Could you please consider posting a review on the platform? Reviews are one of the easiest ways to support the work of authors.***

This feedback will help me continue to write the type of books that will help you get the results you want. So if you enjoyed it, please let me know.

Resources Page

7. Ho, K. Y., Veldhuis, J. D., Johnson, M. L., Furlanetto, R., Evans, W. S., Alberti, K. G., & Thorner, M. O. (1988). Fasting enhances growth hormone secretion and amplifies the complex rhythms of growth hormone secretion in man. *Journal of Clinical Investigation, 81*(4), 968–975. https://doi.org/10.1172/JCI113450

8. Salgin, B., Marcovecchio, M. L., Hill, N., Dunger, D. B., & Frystyk, J. (2012). The effect of prolonged fasting on levels of growth hormone-binding protein and free growth hormone. *Growth Hormone & IGF Research, 22*(2), 76–81. https://doi.org/10.1016/j.ghir.2012.02.003

9. Takahashi, Y., Kipnis, D. M., & Daughaday, W. H. (1968). Growth hormone secretion during sleep. *Journal of Clinical Investigation, 47*(9), 2079–2090. https://doi.org/10.1172/JCI105893

10. Mihaylova, M. M., Cheng, C.-W., Cao, A. Q., Tripathi, S., Mana, M. D., Bauer-Rowe, K. E., ... Yilmaz, Ö. H. (2018). Fasting Activates Fatty Acid Oxidation to Enhance Intestinal Stem Cell Function during Homeostasis and Aging. *Cell Stem Cell, 22*(5), 769-778.e4. https://doi.org/10.1016/j.stem.2018.04.001

11. Kim, H.-S., Patel, K., Muldoon-Jacobs, K., Bisht, K. S., Aykin-Burns, N., Pennington, J. D., ... Gius, D. (2010). SIRT3 Is a Mitochondria-Localized Tumor Suppressor Required for Maintenance of Mitochondrial Integrity and Metabolism during Stress. *Cancer Cell, 17*(1), 41–52. https://doi.org/10.1016/j.ccr.2009.11.023

12. Mattson, M. P., Moehl, K., Ghena, N., Schmaedick, M., & Cheng, A. (2018). Intermittent metabolic switching, neuroplasticity and brain health. *Nature Reviews Neuroscience, 19*(2), 80. https://doi.org/10.1038/nrn.2017.156

13. Zhang, J., Zhan, Z., Li, X., Xing, A., Jiang, C., Chen, Y., ... An, L. (2017). Intermittent Fasting Protects against Alzheimer's Disease Possible through Restoring Aquaporin-4 Polarity. *Frontiers in Molecular Neuroscience, 10.* https://doi.org/10.3389/fnmol.2017.00395

14. de Groot, S., Pijl, H., van der Hoeven, J. J. M., & Kroep, J. R. (2019). Effects of short-term fasting on cancer treatment. *Journal of Experimental & Clinical Cancer Research, 38*(1). https://doi.org/10.1186/s13046-019-1189-9

15. Van der Lee, K. A. J. M., P. H. M. Willemsen, S. Samec, J. Seydoux, A. G. Dulloo, M. M. A. L. Pelsers, J. F. C. Glatz, G. J. Van der Vusse, and M. Van Bilsen (2001). Fasting-induced changes in the expression of genes

controlling substrate metabolism in the rat heart. *J. Lipid Res.*, 42, 1752–1758.

16. Kim, J., Kang, S.-W., Mallilankaraman, K., Baik, S.-H., Lim, J. C., Balaganapathy, P., ... Arumugam, T. V. (2018). Transcriptome analysis reveals intermittent fasting-induced genetic changes in ischemic stroke. *Human Molecular Genetics*, *27*(9), 1497–1513. https://doi.org/10.1093/hmg/ddy057

17. Pilegaard, H., Saltin, B., & Neufer, P. D. (2003). Effect of Short-Term Fasting and Refeeding on Transcriptional Regulation of Metabolic Genes in Human Skeletal Muscle. *Diabetes*, *52*(3), 657–662. https://doi.org/10.2337/diabetes.52.3.657

18. Kassab, S., Abdul-Ghaffar, T., Nagalla, D. S., Sachdeva, U., & Nayar, U. (2004). Interactions between leptin, neuropeptide-Y and insulin with chronic diurnal fasting during Ramadan. *Annals of Saudi Medicine*, *24*(5), 345–349. https://doi.org/10.5144/0256-4947.2004.345

19. Crujeiras, A. B., Goyenechea, E., Abete, I., Lage, M., Carreira, M. C., Martínez, J. A., & Casanueva, F. F. (2010). Weight Regain after a Diet-Induced Loss Is Predicted by Higher Baseline Leptin and Lower Ghrelin Plasma Levels. *The Journal of Clinical Endocrinology & Metabolism*, *95*(11), 5037–5044. https://doi.org/10.1210/jc.2009-2566

20. Berga, S. (2001). Endocrine and chronobiological effects of fasting in women. *Fertility and Sterility, 75*(5), 926–932. https://doi.org/10.1016/s0015-0282(01)01686-7

21. Berga, S. (2001). Endocrine and chronobiological effects of fasting in women. *Fertility and Sterility, 75*(5), 926–932. https://doi.org/10.1016/s0015-0282(01)01686-7

22. Schwalm, C., Jamart, C., Benoit, N., Naslain, D., Prémont, C., Prévet, J., ... Francaux, M. (2015). Activation of autophagy in human skeletal muscle is dependent on exercise intensity and AMPK activation. *The FASEB Journal, 29*(8), 3515–3526. https://doi.org/10.1096/fj.14-267187

23. Chen, F., Bao, H., Xie, H., Tian, G., & Jiang, T. (2018). Heat shock protein expression and autophagy after incomplete thermal ablation and their correlation. *International Journal of Hyperthermia, 36*(1), 95–103. https://doi.org/10.1080/02656736.2018.1536285

24. Martinez-Lopez, N., Garcia-Macia, M., Sahu, S., Athonvarangkul, D., Liebling, E., Merlo, P., ... Singh, R. (2016). Autophagy in the CNS and Periphery Coordinate Lipophagy and Lipolysis in the Brown Adipose Tissue and Liver. *Cell Metabolism, 23*(1), 113–127. https://doi.org/10.1016/j.cmet.2015.10.008

25. Han, J. R., Deng, B., Sun, J., Chen, C. G., Corkey, B. E., Kirkland, J. L., ... Guo, W. (2007). Effects of dietary medium-chain triglyceride on weight loss and insulin

sensitivity in a group of moderately overweight free-living type 2 diabetic Chinese subjects. *Metabolism, 56*(7), 985–991. https://doi.org/10.1016/j.metabol.2007.03.005

26. Abdel-Mohsen, M. A., El-Braky, A. A.-A., Ghazal, A. A. E.-R., & Shamseya, M. M. (2018). Autophagy, apoptosis, vitamin D, and vitamin D receptor in hepatocellular carcinoma associated with hepatitis C virus. *Medicine, 97*(12), e0172. https://doi.org/10.1097/MD.0000000000010172

27. Sarkar, S., Floto, R. A., Berger, Z., Imarisio, S., Cordenier, A., Pasco, M., ... Rubinsztein, D. C. (2005). Lithium induces autophagy by inhibiting inositol monophosphatase. *The Journal of Cell Biology, 170*(7), 1101–1111. https://doi.org/10.1083/jcb.200504035

28. Jang, J., Jung, Y., Seo, S. J., Kim, S.-M., Shim, Y. J., Cho, S. H., ... Yoon, Y. (2017). Berberine activates AMPK to suppress proteolytic processing, nuclear translocation and target DNA binding of SREBP-1c in 3T3-L1 adipocytes. *Molecular Medicine Reports, 15*(6), 4139–4147. https://doi.org/10.3892/mmr.2017.651324

29. Jang, J., Jung, Y., Seo, S. J., Kim, S.-M., Shim, Y. J., Cho, S. H., ... Yoon, Y. (2017). Berberine activates AMPK to suppress proteolytic processing, nuclear translocation and target DNA binding of SREBP-1c in 3T3-L1

adipocytes. *Molecular Medicine Reports, 15*(6), 4139–4147. https://doi.org/10.3892/mmr.2017.6513

30. Aliev, G., Liu, J., Shenk, J. C., Fischbach, K., Pacheco, G. J., Chen, S. G., ... Ames, B. N. (2008). Neuronal mitochondrial amelioration by feeding acetyl-L-carnitine and lipoic acid to aged rats. *Journal of Cellular and Molecular Medicine, 13*(2), 320–333. https://doi.org/10.1111/j.1582-4934.2008.00324.x

31. Chan, Y. L., Saad, S., Al-Odat, I., Oliver, B. G., Pollock, C., Jones, N. M., & Chen, H. (2017). Maternal L-Carnitine Supplementation Improves Brain Health in Offspring from Cigarette Smoke Exposed Mothers. *Frontiers in Molecular Neuroscience, 10.* https://doi.org/10.3389/fnmol.2017.0003327

32. Lee, K. R., Midgette, Y., & Shah, R. (2018). Fish Oil Derived Omega 3 Fatty Acids Suppress Adipose NLRP3 Inflammasome Signaling in Human Obesity. *Journal of the Endocrine Society, 3*(3), 504–515. https://doi.org/10.1210/js.2018-00220

33. Mazereeuw, G., Herrmann, N., Oh, P. I., Ma, D. W. L., Wang, C. T., Kiss, A., & Lanctôt, K. 9L. (2016). Omega-3 Fatty Acids, Depressive Symptoms, and Cognitive

Performance in Patients With Coronary Artery Disease. *Journal of Clinical Psychopharmacology, 36*(5), 436–444. https://doi.org/10.1097/JCP.0000000000000565

34. Poulose, S., Bielinski, D. F., & Shukkit-Hale, B. (2011, April 1). Neuronal housekeeping via activation of autophagy by blueberry, strawberry, acai berry and walnut extracts. Retrieved November 4, 2019, from https://www.fasebj.org/doi/abs/10.1096/fasebj.25.1_su pplement.213.8

35. Kim, H.-S., Quon, M. J., & Kim, J. (2014). New insights into the mechanisms of polyphenols beyond antioxidant properties; lessons from the green tea polyphenol, epigallocatechin 3-gallate. *Redox Biology, 2,* 187–195. https://doi.org/10.1016/j.redox.2013.12.022

36. Tian, J., Popal, M. S., Liu, Y., Gao, R., Lyu, S., Chen, K., & Liu, Y. (2019). Ginkgo Biloba Leaf Extract Attenuates Atherosclerosis in Streptozotocin-Induced Diabetic ApoE-/- Mice by Inhibiting Endoplasmic Reticulum Stress via Restoration of Autophagy through the mTOR Signaling Pathway. *Oxidative Medicine and Cellular Longevity, 2019,* 1–19. https://doi.org/10.1155/2019/8134678

37. Zhu, Y., & Bu, S. (2017). Curcumin Induces Autophagy, Apoptosis, and Cell Cycle Arrest in Human Pancreatic Cancer Cells. *Evidence-Based Complementary and Alternative Medicine, 2017*, 1–13. https://doi.org/10.1155/2017/5787218

38. Araveti, P. B., & Srivastava, A. (2019). Curcumin induced oxidative stress causes autophagy and apoptosis in bovine leucocytes transformed by Theileria annulata. *Cell Death Discovery, 5*(1). https://doi.org/10.1038/s41420-019-0180-8

39. Pietrocola, F., Malik, S. A., Mariño, G., Vacchelli, E., Senovilla, L., chaba, kariman, ... Kroemer, G. (2014). Coffee induces autophagy in vivo. *Cell Cycle, 13*(12), 1987–1994. https://doi.org/10.4161/cc.28929

40. Mathew, T. S., Ferris, R. K., Downs, R. M., Kinsey, S. T., & Baumgarner, B. L. (2014). Caffeine promotes autophagy in skeletal muscle cells by increasing the calcium-dependent activation of AMP-activated protein kinase. *Biochemical and Biophysical Research Communications, 453*(3), 411–418. https://doi.org/10.1016/j.bbrc.2014.09.094

41. Huang, S., Mao, J., Ding, K., Zhou, Y., Zeng, X., Yang, W., ... Pei, G. (2017). Polysaccharides from Ganoderma

lucidum Promote Cognitive Function and Neural Progenitor Proliferation in Mouse Model of Alzheimer's Disease. *Stem Cell Reports, 8*(1), 84–94. https://doi.org/10.1016/j.stemcr.2016.12.007

42. Hung, J.-Y., Hsu, Y.-L., Li, C.-T., Ko, Y.-C., Ni, W.-C., Huang, M.-S., & Kuo, P.-L. (2009). 6-Shogaol, an Active Constituent of Dietary Ginger, Induces Autophagy by Inhibiting the AKT/mTOR Pathway in Human Non-Small Cell Lung Cancer A549 Cells. *Journal of Agricultural and Food Chemistry, 57*(20), 9809–9816. https://doi.org/10.1021/jf902315e

43. Tavera-Mendoza, L. E., Westerling, T., Libby, E., Marusyk, A., Cato, L., Cassani, R., ... Brown, M. (2017). Vitamin D receptor regulates autophagy in the normal mammary gland and in luminal breast cancer cells. *Proceedings of the National Academy of Sciences, 114*(11), E2186–E2194. https://doi.org/10.1073/pnas.1615015114

44. Nishikawa, T., Tsuno, N. H., Okaji, Y., Shuno, Y., Sasaki, K., Hongo, K., ... Nagawa, H. (2009). Inhibition of Autophagy Potentiates Sulforaphane-Induced Apoptosis in Human Colon Cancer Cells. *Annals of Surgical*

Oncology, 17(2), 592–602.
https://doi.org/10.1245/s10434-009-0696-x

45. Yang, F., Wang, F., Liu, Y., Wang, S., Li, X., Huang, Y., ... Cao, C. (2018). Sulforaphane induces autophagy by inhibition of HDAC6-mediated PTEN activation in triple negative breast cancer cells. *Life Sciences, 213*, 149–157. https://doi.org/10.1016/j.lfs.2018.10.034

46. Wen, M., Wu, J., Luo, H., & Zhang, H. (2012). Galangin Induces Autophagy through Upregulation of p53 in HepG2 Cells. *Pharmacology, 89*(5–6), 247–255. https://doi.org/10.1159/000337041

47. Alirezaei, M., Kemball, C. C., Flynn, C. T., Wood, M. R., Whitton, J. L., & Kiosses, W. B. (2010). Short-term fasting induces profound neuronal autophagy. *Autophagy, 6*(6), 702–710. https://doi.org/10.4161/auto.6.6.12376

48. M L Hartman, J D Veldhuis, M L Johnson, M M Lee, K G Alberti, E Samojlik, M O Thorner (1992). Augmented growth hormone (GH) secretory burst frequency and amplitude mediate enhanced GH secretion during a two-day fast in normal men. *The Journal of Clinical*

Endocrinology & Metabolism, 74(4), Pages 757–765, https://doi.org/10.1210/jcem.74.4.1548337

49. Klein, S., Sakurai, Y., Romijn, J. A., & Carroll, R. M. (1993). Progressive alterations in lipid and glucose metabolism during short-term fasting in young adult men. *American Journal of Physiology-Endocrinology and Metabolism*, 265(5), E801–E806. https://doi.org/10.1152/ajpendo.1993.265.5.E801

50. Cheng, C.-W., Adams, G. B., Perin, L., Wei, M., Zhou, X., Lam, B. S., ... Longo, V. D. (2014). Prolonged Fasting Reduces IGF-1/PKA to Promote Hematopoietic-Stem-Cell-Based Regeneration and Reverse Immunosuppression. *Cell Stem Cell*, 14(6), 810–823. https://doi.org/10.1016/j.stem.2014.04.014

51. Trepanowski, J. F., Kroeger, C. M., Barnosky, A., Klempel, M. C., Bhutani, S., Hoddy, K. K., ... Varady, K. A. (2017). Effect of Alternate-Day Fasting on Weight Loss, Weight Maintenance, and Cardioprotection Among Metabolically Healthy Obese Adults. *JAMA Internal Medicine*, 177(7), 930. https://doi.org/10.1001/jamainternmed.2017.0936

52. Halberg, N., Henriksen, M., Söderhamn, N., Stallknecht, B., Ploug, T., Schjerling, P., & Dela, F. (2005). Effect of intermittent fasting and refeeding on insulin action in healthy men. *Journal of Applied Physiology*, *99*(6), 2128–2136. https://doi.org/10.1152/japplphysiol.00683.2005

53. Kim, K. R., Nam, S. Y., Song, Y. D., Lim, S. K., Lee, H. C., & Huh, K. B. (1999). Low-Dose Growth Hormone Treatment with Diet Restriction Accelerates Body Fat Loss, Exerts Anabolic Effect and Improves Growth Hormone Secretory Dysfunction in Obese Adults. *Hormone Research in Paediatrics*, *51*(2), 78–84. https://doi.org/10.1159/000023319

54. Gabel, K., Hoddy, K. K., Haggerty, N., Song, J., Kroeger, C. M., Trepanowski, J. F., … Varady, K. A. (2018). Effects of 8-hour time restricted feeding on body weight and metabolic disease risk factors in obese adults: A pilot study. *Nutrition and Healthy Aging*, *4*(4), 345–353. https://doi.org/10.3233/NHA-170036

55. Betz, M. J., Bielohuby, M., Mauracher, B., Abplanalp, W., Müller, H.-H., Pieper, K., … Slawik, M. (2012). Isoenergetic Feeding of Low Carbohydrate-High Fat Diets Does Not Increase Brown Adipose Tissue

Thermogenic Capacity in Rats. *PLoS ONE, 7*(6), e38997. https://doi.org/10.1371/journal.pone.0038997

56. Myers, C. A., Martin, C. K., & Apolzan, J. W. (2018). Food cravings and body weight. *Current Opinion in Endocrinology & Diabetes and Obesity, 25*(5), 298–302. https://doi.org/10.1097/MED.0000000000000434

57. Martin, C. K., Rosenbaum, D., Han, H., Geiselman, P. J., Wyatt, H. R., Hill, J. O., ... Foster, G. D. (2011). Change in Food Cravings, Food Preferences, and Appetite During a Low-Carbohydrate and Low-Fat Diet. *Obesity, 19*(10), 1963–1970. https://doi.org/10.1038/oby.2011.62

58. Hallam, J., Boswell, R. G., DeVito, E. E., & Kober, H. (2016). Gender-related Differences in Food Craving and Obesity. *The Yale journal of biology and medicine, 89*(2), 161–173.

59. Ravussin, E., Beyl, R. A., Poggiogalle, E., Hsia, D. S., & Peterson, C. M. (2019). Early Time-Restricted Feeding Reduces Appetite and Increases Fat Oxidation But Does Not Affect Energy Expenditure in Humans. *Obesity, 27*(8), 1244–1254. https://doi.org/10.1002/oby.22518

60. Tinsley, G. M., Forsse, J. S., Butler, N. K., Paoli, A., Bane, A. A., La Bounty, P. M., ... Grandjean, P. W. (2016). Time-restricted feeding in young men performing resistance training: A randomized controlled trial. *European Journal of Sport Science, 17*(2), 200–207. https://doi.org/10.1080/17461391.2016.1223173

61. Velloso, C. P. (2008). Regulation of muscle mass by growth hormone and IGF-I. *British Journal of Pharmacology, 154*(3), 557–568. https://doi.org/10.1038/bjp.2008.153

62. Lee, D., Bareja, A., Bartlett, D., & White, J. (2019). Autophagy as a Therapeutic Target to Enhance Aged Muscle Regeneration. *Cells, 8*(2), 183. https://doi.org/10.3390/cells8020183

63. Hutchison, A. T., Liu, B., Wood, R. E., Vincent, A. D., Thompson, C. H., O'Callaghan, N. J., ... Heilbronn, L. K. (2018). Effects of Intermittent Versus Continuous Energy Intakes on Insulin Sensitivity and Metabolic Risk in Women with Overweight. *Obesity, 27*(1), 50–58. https://doi.org/10.1002/oby.22345

64. Kosacka, J., Nowicki, M., Paeschke, S., Baum, P., Blüher, M., & Klöting, N. (2018). Up-regulated autophagy: as a

protective factor in adipose tissue of WOKW rats with metabolic syndrome. *Diabetology & Metabolic Syndrome, 10*(1). https://doi.org/10.1186/s13098-018-0317-6

65. Fernández, Á. F., Bárcena, C., Martínez-García, G. G., Tamargo-Gómez, I., Suárez, M. F., Pietrocola, F., ... Mariño, G. (2017). Autophagy couteracts weight gain, lipotoxicity and pancreatic β-cell death upon hypercaloric pro-diabetic regimens. *Cell Death & Disease, 8*(8), e2970. https://doi.org/10.1038/cddis.2017.373

66. Deutsches Zentrum fuer Diabetesforschung DZD. (2019, July 2). Promising approach: Prevent diabetes with intermittent fasting. *ScienceDaily*. Retrieved November 4, 2019 from www.sciencedaily.com/releases/2019/07/190702152749.htm

67. **63** https://www.ncbi.nlm.nih.gov/pmc/articles/PMC5479440/

68. Yang, J. S., Lu, C. C., Kuo, S. C., Hsu, Y. M., Tsai, S. C., Chen, S. Y., ... Tsai, F. J. (2017). Autophagy and its link

to type II diabetes mellitus. *BioMedicine, 7*(2), 8. doi:10.1051/bmdcn/2017070201

69. Barnosky, A. R., Hoddy, K. K., Unterman, T. G., & Varady, K. A. (2014). Intermittent fasting vs daily calorie restriction for type 2 diabetes prevention: a review of human findings. *Translational Research, 164*(4), 302–311. https://doi.org/10.1016/j.trsl.2014.05.013

70. Mattson, M. P., Moehl, K., Ghena, N., Schmaedick, M., & Cheng, A. (2018). Intermittent metabolic switching, neuroplasticity and brain health. *Nature reviews. Neuroscience, 19*(2), 63–80. doi:10.1038/nrn.2017.156

71. Katsurada, K., & Yada, T. (2016). Neural effects of gut- and brain-derived glucagon-like peptide-1 and its receptor agonist. *Journal of Diabetes Investigation, 7*, 64–69. https://doi.org/10.1111/jdi.12464

72. Hartman, A. L., Rubenstein, J. E., & Kossoff, E. H. (2013). Intermittent fasting: a "new" historical strategy for controlling seizures?. *Epilepsy research, 104*(3), 275–279. doi:10.1016/j.eplepsyres.2012.10.011

73. Zhang, L., & Wang, H. (2018). Autophagy in Traumatic Brain Injury: A New Target for Therapeutic Intervention. *Frontiers in molecular neuroscience, 11,* 190. doi:10.3389/fnmol.2018.00190

74. Davis, L. M., Pauly, J. R., Readnower, R. D., Rho, J. M., & Sullivan, P. G. (2008). Fasting is neuroprotective following traumatic brain injury. *Journal of Neuroscience Research, 86*(8), 1812–1822. https://doi.org/10.1002/jnr.21628

75. Mattson, M. P., Longo, V. D., & Harvie, M. (2017). Impact of intermittent fasting on health and disease processes. *Ageing research reviews, 39,* 46–58. doi:10.1016/j.arr.2016.10.005

76. Servante, J., Estranero, J., Meijer, L., Layfield, R., & Grundy, R. (2018). Chemical modulation of autophagy as an adjunct to chemotherapy in childhood and adolescent brain tumors. *Oncotarget, 9*(81), 35266–35277. doi:10.18632/oncotarget.26186

77. Bossy, B., Perkins, G., & Bossy-Wetzel, E. (2008). Clearing the brain's cobwebs: the role of autophagy in neuroprotection. *Current neuropharmacology, 6*(2), 97–101. doi:10.2174/157015908784533897

78. Mattson, M. P., Moehl, K., Ghena, N., Schmaedick, M., & Cheng, A. (2018). Intermittent metabolic switching, neuroplasticity and brain health. *Nature reviews. Neuroscience, 19*(2), 63–80. doi:10.1038/nrn.2017.156

79. Mattson, M. P., Moehl, K., Ghena, N., Schmaedick, M., & Cheng, A. (2018). Intermittent metabolic switching, neuroplasticity and brain health. *Nature reviews. Neuroscience, 19*(2), 63–80. doi:10.1038/nrn.2017.156

80. Krupczak-Hollis, K., Wang, X., Dennewitz, M. B., & Costa, R. H. (2003). Growth hormone stimulates proliferation of old-aged regenerating liver through forkhead box m1b. *Hepatology, 38*(6), 1552–1562. https://doi.org/10.1016/j.hep.2003.08.052

81. Müller-Wiefel, D., Frisch, H., Tulassay, T., Bell, L., & Zadik, Z. (2010). Treatment of growth failure with growth hormone in children with chronic kidney disease: an open-label long-term study. *Clinical Nephrology, 74*(08), 97–105. https://doi.org/10.5414/cnp74097

82. Caramés, B., Taniguchi, N., Otsuki, S., Blanco, F. J., & Lotz, M. (2010). Autophagy is a protective mechanism in normal cartilage, and its aging-related loss is linked with

cell death and osteoarthritis. *Arthritis & Rheumatism, 62*(3), 791–801. https://doi.org/10.1002/art.27305

83. Yin, X., Zhou, C., Li, J., Liu, R., Shi, B., Yuan, Q., & Zou, S. (2019). Autophagy in bone homeostasis and the onset of osteoporosis. *Bone Research, 7*(1). https://doi.org/10.1038/s41413-019-0058-7

84. Mattson, M. P. (2008). Dietary factors, hormesis and health. *Ageing Research Reviews, 7*(1), 43–48. https://doi.org/10.1016/j.arr.2007.08.004

85. Martinez-Lopez, N., Athonvarangkul, D., & Singh, R. (2015). Autophagy and Aging. *Longevity Genes,* 73–87. https://doi.org/10.1007/978-1-4939-2404-2_3

86. Ma, S., & Suzuki, K. (2019). Keto-Adaptation and Endurance Exercise Capacity, Fatigue Recovery, and Exercise-Induced Muscle and Organ Damage Prevention: A Narrative Review. *Sports, 7*(2), 40. https://doi.org/10.3390/sports7020040

87. Malinowski, B., Zalewska, K., Węsierska, A., Sokołowska, M. M., Socha, M., Liczner, G., ... Wiciński, M. (2019). Intermittent Fasting in Cardiovascular Disorders—An

Overview. *Nutrients, 11*(3), 673.
https://doi.org/10.3390/nu11030673

88. Sutton, E. F., Beyl, R., Early, K. S., Cefalu, W. T.,
Ravussin, E., & Peterson, C. M. (2018). Early Time-
Restricted Feeding Improves Insulin Sensitivity, Blood
Pressure, and Oxidative Stress Even without Weight Loss
in Men with Prediabetes. *Cell Metabolism, 27*(6), 1212-
1221.e3. https://doi.org/10.1016/j.cmet.2018.04.010

89. Santos, H. O., & Macedo, R. C. O. (2018). Impact of
intermittent fasting on the lipid profile: Assessment
associated with diet and weight loss. *Clinical Nutrition
ESPEN, 24*, 14–21.
https://doi.org/10.1016/j.clnesp.2018.01.002

90. Luo, Y., Ma, X., Shen, Y., Hao, Y., Hu, Y., Xiao, Y., ... Jia,
W. (2014). Positive Relationship between Serum Low-
Density Lipoprotein Cholesterol Levels and Visceral Fat
in a Chinese Nondiabetic Population. *PLoS ONE, 9*(11),
e112715. https://doi.org/10.1371/journal.pone.0112715

91. Soudijn, W., van Wijngaarden, I., & IJzerman, A. P.
(2007). Nicotinic acid receptor subtypes and their
ligands. *Medicinal Research Reviews, 27*(3), 417–433.
https://doi.org/10.1002/med.20102

92. Yang, M., Zhang, Y., & Ren, J. (2018). Autophagic Regulation of Lipid Homeostasis in Cardiometabolic Syndrome. *Frontiers in cardiovascular medicine, 5,* 38. doi:10.3389/fcvm.2018.00038

93. Bragazzi, N. L., Sellami, M., Salem, I., Conic, R., Kimak, M., Pigatto, P., & Damiani, G. (2019). Fasting and Its Impact on Skin Anatomy, Physiology, and Physiopathology: A Comprehensive Review of the Literature. *Nutrients, 11*(2), 249. doi:10.3390/nu11020249

94. Furmli, S., Elmasry, R., Ramos, M., & Fung, J. (2018). Therapeutic use of intermittent fasting for people with type 2 diabetes as an alternative to insulin. *BMJ Case Reports,* bcr-2017-221854. https://doi.org/10.1136/bcr-2017-221854

95. Liu, H., Javaheri, A., Godar, R. J., Murphy, J., Ma, X., Rohatgi, N., ... Diwan, A. (2017). Intermittent fasting preserves beta-cell mass in obesity-induced diabetes via the autophagy-lysosome pathway. *Autophagy, 13*(11), 1952–1968. https://doi.org/10.1080/15548627.2017.1368596

96. Kuballa, P., Nolte, W. M., Castoreno, A. B., & Xavier, R. J. (2012). Autophagy and the Immune System. *Annual*

Review of Immunology, 30(1), 611–646.
https://doi.org/10.1146/annurev-immunol-020711-074948

97. Valdor, R., & Macian, F. (2012). Autophagy and the regulation of the immune response. *Pharmacological Research, 66*(6), 475–483.
https://doi.org/10.1016/j.phrs.2012.10.003

98. Bruning, P. F., Bonfrèr, J. M. G., van Noord, P. A. H., Hart, A. A. M., de Jong-Bakker, M., & Nooijen, W. J. (1992). Insulin resistance and breast-cancer risk. *International Journal of Cancer, 52*(4), 511–516.
https://doi.org/10.1002/ijc.2910520402

99. Tsugane, S., & Inoue, M. (2010). Insulin resistance and cancer: Epidemiological evidence. *Cancer Science, 101*(5), 1073–1079.
https://doi.org/10.1111/j.1349-7006.2010.01521.x

100. Galluzzi, L., Pietrocola, F., Bravo-San Pedro, J. M., Amaravadi, R. K., Baehrecke, E. H., Cecconi, F., ... Kroemer, G. (2015). Autophagy in malignant transformation and cancer progression. *The EMBO journal, 34*(7), 856–880. doi:10.15252/embj.201490784

101. de Groot, S., Pijl, H., van der Hoeven, J., & Kroep, J. R. (2019). Effects of short-term fasting on cancer treatment. *Journal of experimental & clinical cancer research : CR, 38*(1), 209. doi:10.1186/s13046-019-1189-9

102. Jylhävä, J., Pedersen, N. L., & Hägg, S. (2017). Biological Age Predictors. *EBioMedicine, 21,* 29–36. doi:10.1016/j.ebiom.2017.03.046

103. Chauhan, A. K., & Mallick, B. N. (2019). Association between autophagy and rapid eye movement sleep loss-associated neurodegenerative and patho-physio-behavioral changes. *Sleep Medicine, 63,* 29–37. https://doi.org/10.1016/j.sleep.2019.04.019

104. Ashar, F. N., Moes, A., Moore, A. Z., Grove, M. L., Chaves, P., Coresh, J., ... Arking, D. E. (2015). Association of mitochondrial DNA levels with frailty and all-cause mortality. *Journal of molecular medicine (Berlin, Germany), 93*(2), 177–186. doi:10.1007/s00109-014-1233-3

105. Glazier, J. D., Hayes, D., Hussain, S., D'Souza, S. W., Whitcombe, J., Heazell, A., & Ashton, N. (2018). The effect of Ramadan fasting during pregnancy on perinatal outcomes: a systematic review and meta-analysis. *BMC*

pregnancy and childbirth, 18(1), 421.
doi:10.1186/s12884-018-2048-y

106.   Ganesan, K., Habboush, Y., & Sultan, S. (2018).
Intermittent Fasting: The Choice for a Healthier
Lifestyle. *Cureus, 10*(7), e2947. doi:10.7759/cureus.2947

107.   Nair, P. M., & Khawale, P. G. (2016). Role of
therapeutic fasting in women's health: An
overview. *Journal of mid-life health, 7*(2), 61–64.
doi:10.4103/0976-7800.185325

108.   Leiper, J. B., Molla, A. M., & Molla, A. M. (2003).
Effects on health of fluid restriction during fasting in
Ramadan. *European Journal of Clinical
Nutrition, 57*(S2), S30–S38.
https://doi.org/10.1038/sj.ejcn.1601899

109.   Arguin, H., Dionne, I. J., Sénéchal, M., Bouchard, D.
R., Carpentier, A. C., Ardilouze, J.-L., … Brochu, M.
(2012). Short- and long-term effects of continuous versus
intermittent restrictive diet approaches on body
composition and the metabolic profile in overweight and
obese postmenopausal women. *Menopause: The Journal
of The North American Menopause Society, 19*(8), 870–
876. https://doi.org/10.1097/gme.0b013e318250a287

110.   Hlebowicz, J., Darwiche, G., Björgell, O., & Almér, L.-
O. (2007). Effect of apple cider vinegar on delayed
gastric emptying in patients with type 1 diabetes

mellitus: a pilot study. *BMC Gastroenterology, 7*(1). https://doi.org/10.1186/1471-230X-7-46

111.   Kondo, T., Kishi, M., Fushimi, T., & Kaga, T. (2009). Acetic Acid Upregulates the Expression of Genes for Fatty Acid Oxidation Enzymes in Liver To Suppress Body Fat Accumulation. *Journal of Agricultural and Food Chemistry, 57*(13), 5982–5986. https://doi.org/10.1021/jf900470c

CPSIA information can be obtained
at www.ICGtesting.com
Printed in the USA
LVHW080348090621
689770LV00002B/18